THE PACIFIC WAR UNCENSORED

ectorate

Erro

AUST.

Harold Cward.

(Signature of Correspondent)

Thumbprint.

The Pacific War Uncensored

A War Correspondent's Unvarnished
Account of the Fight Against Japan

BY
HAROLD GUARD

EDITED BY
JOHN TRING

CASEMATE
Philadelphia & Newbury

Published in the United States of America and Great Britain in 2011 by
CASEMATE PUBLISHERS
908 Darby Road, Havertown, PA 19083
and
17 Cheap Street, Newbury RG14 5DD

Copyright 2011 © Harold Guard and John Tring

ISBN 978-1-61200-064-0
Digital Edition: ISBN 978-1-61200-081-7

Cataloging-in-publication data is available from the Library of Congress
and the British Library.

10 9 8 7 6 5 4 3 2 1

Printed and bound in the United States of America.

For a complete list of Casemate titles please contact:

CASEMATE PUBLISHERS (US)
Telephone (610) 853-9131, Fax (610) 853-9146
E-mail: casemate@casematepublishing.com

CASEMATE PUBLISHERS (UK)
Telephone (01635) 231091, Fax (01635) 41619
E-mail: casemate-uk@casematepublishing.co.uk

Contents

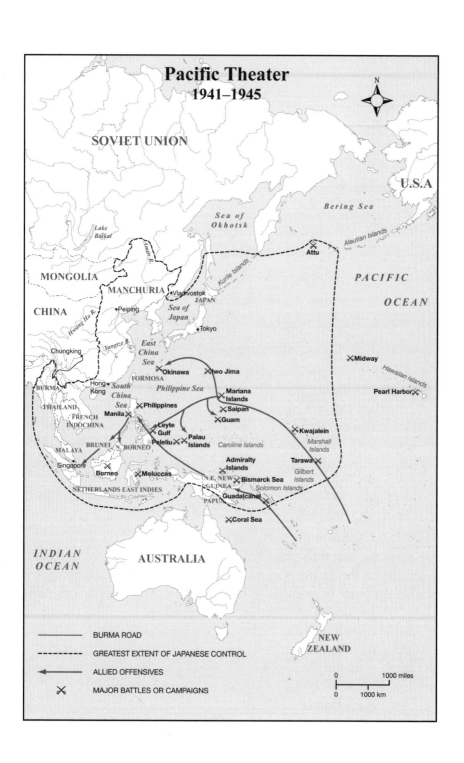

Pacific Theater
1941–1945

N

SOVIET UNION

U.S.A

Bering Sea

Lake Baikal

MONGOLIA

MANCHURIA •Vladivostok

JAPAN

Sea of Okhotsk

Kurile Islands

✕ Attu

Aleutian Islands

PACIFIC

OCEAN

CHINA

•Peiping

Hwang Ho R.

Amur R.

Sea of Japan

•Tokyo

Yangtze R.

Chungking

East China Sea

✕Okinawa   ✕Iwo Jima

FORMOSA

Hong• Kong

BURMA

South China Sea

Philippine Sea

✕Midway

Hawaiian Islands

Pearl Harbor✕

THAILAND

FRENCH INDOCHINA

✕Philippines

Manila✕

Mariana ✕ Islands

✕Saipan

✕Guam

MALAYA

BRUNEI

N. BORNEO

✕Leyte
✕ Gulf

Peleliu✕✕ Palau
Islands

Caroline Islands

✕ Kwajalein

Marshall Islands

Singapore

Borneo   ✕Moluccas

Admiralty ✕ Islands

Tarawa ✕

Gilbert Islands

NETHERLANDS EAST INDIES

N.E. NEW✕ ✕Bismarck Sea
GUINEA

PAPUA

✕Guadalcanal

Solomon Islands

✕Coral Sea

INDIAN OCEAN

AUSTRALIA

NEW
ZEALAND

———— BURMA ROAD

- - - - - GREATEST EXTENT OF JAPANESE CONTROL

⟵ ALLIED OFFENSIVES

✕ MAJOR BATTLES OR CAMPAIGNS

0   1000 miles

0   1000 km

Introduction

I n March 1942, my grandfather, Harold Guard, arrived in Sydney, Australia, having narrowly escaped the Japanese forces invading Singapore and Java. He was a war correspondent working for an American news agency, the United Press, and at the time was acclaimed by the Australian press as being one of the top four newspapermen covering the war in the Pacific, as he often reported from perilous situations at the front line. Shortly after his arrival in Australia, a New York publishing house sent Harold a telegram, asking him to write a book "immediately" about his experiences, which he ignored, because as far as he was concerned the war was only three months old and far from finished.

Over the next three years Harold was to have many more adventures reporting on the Pacific War, including firsthand experiences flying with the US Air Force on twenty-two bombing missions, camping with Allied forces in the jungles of New Guinea, and taking part in attacks from amphibious landing craft on enemy occupied territory. He also travelled into the undeveloped areas of Australia's Northern Territories to report on the construction of the airbases that were being built in preparation for defending the country against the advancing Japanese forces.

What made Harold's achievements even more remarkable was that he was disabled and had to walk with a stiff right leg, which was due to an accident that he'd had while working as a naval engineer in the British navy. Harold had followed in the footsteps of his father and older brother by joining the Royal Navy when he was 16, where he trained as an engine room artificer. During his service he worked mainly on submarines, which at the time appeared to be at a developmental stage, and was a crewmember of the ill-fated K13 that sank to the bottom of the Gareloch in Rosyth, Scotland. The K13 was a special type of submarine that could operate on the surface as well as under water, but unfortunately, it sank due to its funnels not being closed properly. Despite this horrendous experience, Harold was not put off from serving on submarines, and in 1917 took part in a mission to the Baltic in support of the White Russian and international forces opposing the new Bolshevik regime. Their objective was to attack Russian warships inside Kronstadt harbour, which was located on Kotlin Island near the Gulf of Finland. It turned out to be a great success, and led to the award of Victoria Crosses to the fleet's commanders, and recommendations for decoration of the submarine crews.

Following this adventure Harold was assigned to another submarine, the H23, which was a training boat for senior officers. His duties included demonstrating how various procedures were to be carried out; among his students were the young lieutenants Lord Louis Mountbatten and Prince George the Duke of Kent. In 1922, as the government aimed to reduce public expenditure, especially redundancies in the armed forces (known as the Geddes Axe), Harold volunteered for service on the K-class submarine, which had a reputation for being accident-prone. The craft that he was assigned to was the K22—the same K13 model that had sunk to the bottom of the Gareloch in Scotland. Harold felt that he had little choice if he wanted to continue his navy career, and in spite of all the adverse publicity surrounding the vessel, he enrolled for service on it. During this time he learned how to correct a fault with the steering mechanism, which, little did he know at the time, would prove to be an invaluable skill many years later when reporting from an amphibious landing craft in the Pacific. Harold was eventually promoted to Chief ERA (Engine Room Artificer) of the first O class submarine, called *Osiris*. Following several trials, *Osiris* was ready to be commissioned, but before this could happen Harold met with an accident that resulted in him being invalided out of the navy. His right kneecap was completely shattered, and following surgery he was left with a stiff leg that he was unable to bend.

After his naval career came to an end he sought a new future in the Far East with his wife Marie, who was an army schoolmistress soon to be stationed in Hong Kong. Harold tried his hand at a variety of jobs before eventually establishing himself in a career as a newspaperman working for the United Press. When war broke out in the Pacific in 1941, he found himself part of the news corps run by the British government's Ministry of Information based in Singapore. Amongst his counterparts, Harold had the unique status of being an Englishman walking with a characteristic heavy limp while wearing an American army uniform. In fact, in many of the prefaces to the articles that he wrote, he was always referred to as an American correspondent, but no mention was ever made about his stiff right leg. This may have also been due to him not drawing attention to it, and just pursuing whatever story might be developing at the time.

He always strived to find out the truth about what was actually happening in the battlefield, and this often brought him into conflict with the army censors at the Ministry of Information. Harold's adventures also brought him into direct contact with some very influential figures, such as Gordon Bennett, General MacArthur, and once more, Lord Louis Mountbatten.

Harold returned to Britain towards the end of the war, where he continued to work for the United Press up until 1959. Unfortunately he had ill health during the later part of his life, and suffered from macular degeneration that left him almost totally blind. As a youngster I would spend many summer holidays with him and my grandmother, and on many occasions would listen to him recount his tales. In 1976 my parents bought him a cassette recorder so that he could record his experiences, and after his death in 1986 these were stored away by my grandmother and not seen again for many years.

I always had it in mind that one day I would retell his story, and after my grandmother passed away in 2001, I managed to locate the cassettes. To my amazement, in spite of the cassettes being over twenty years old, they still played. Since then I have undertaken the task of editing his work by taking dictation from his tapes, and also reading through some of the stories he wrote that I believe were his early attempts at starting a book.

The majority of this book is an exact replica of Harold's own words, and free from the censorship that so often frustrated him. It provides a firsthand account of the conflict in the Far East, with details of the combat that took place in the jungle, air and at sea. It begins with him recounting his accident on the *Osiris* submarine that dramatically changed the direction of his life and led him into many adventures.

—*John Tring*

Harold with the L8 submarine crew (second row, far right), with whom he took part in patrols of the China seas in 1926. *Author collection*

CHAPTER ONE

Osiris

*O*siris was commissioned to go out to the China station, and due to leave Plymouth in Devon on the day of the famous horse race, the Derby, 4th June 1929. Coincidentally, the favourite for the Derby was a horse also called Osiris, so it was natural that all the crew had a bet on it. We were docked further down the south coast at Fort Blockhouse in Portsmouth, waiting to start our journey. I started the port engine by opening the main airline valve, and as soon as I had done this there was a terrific explosion, the force from which threw me back onto the floor, filling the engine room with choking sulphurous fumes. I tried to struggle to my feet, slipping on the steel plates, which were by now covered with a mixture of oil and somebody's guts. As I did so, I noticed that people around me had also been thrown backwards, and there was an intense pain running through my right leg.

It had only been a year earlier that I had first been called to see Commander Lindsey, who told me that there was a new class of submarines to be built at the Vickers Yard in the northwest of England at Barrow-in-Furness, Cumbria. The submarines were called the O Class, and Commander Lindsey, who was to be in charge of the works, wanted me to be his Chief ERA. He wanted me to go up to Barrow-in-Furness to do what was called a "stand-by-job," which involved overseeing the building of the submarines. I was about to sign on for my second period of service with the navy, and I felt extremely proud that I had been promoted to such a position.

I had comfortable lodgings in Barrow-in-Furness and felt extremely privileged, as I was getting seventeen shillings per day during a time when Britain was experiencing a severe depression, known as the "Great Slump." The job was very interesting, and involved me checking through all the blueprints for the new craft. The first submarine was to be called the *Osiris*, and I was not completely happy with some of the materials being used in the construction, which included aluminium for the engine pistons. Also, the engine layout was very complicated, which made some of the parts very difficult to access. Finally though, the first trial trips could be made, and *Osiris* sailed to Campbeltown in Scotland. It dived well, but hairline cracks were found in the valve seating of our air compressors, and so we took the *Osiris* back to Barrow-in-Furness to be fixed. Then a problem was found with the engines, and the gears in the engine had to be dismantled so that the repair work could be carried out. More trials were then conducted in Plymouth, back on the south coast of England, and at last everything appeared to be satisfactory.

Now though, I found myself on the engine room floor in *Osiris*, with a searing pain running through my right leg. The first person to arrive at the scene was the coxswain, who was called Joe Elvin. Part of Joe's responsibilities also included him being the ship's doctor, and he held a lamp over me to try and find his way round in the dark as the lights had gone out. Joe looked over the mushy, bloody pulp that remained of my right leg, and said, "Looks more like a dog's dinner to me." He did his best to make me comfortable, and poured half a pint of navy rum down my throat.

Then somebody else came. More lights and crewmates stepped carefully over me as they carried sagging bodies through the engine room bulkhead door. Joe handed me another cup full of rum and had one himself, just to keep himself from feeling faint. Bracing himself, he did his best to put the pieces of my leg together, and then hastily lashed it all tight and tidy in a canvas roll before trussing me up in an emergency litter until I looked like an Egyptian mummy. A stretcher was brought, and I was carried through to the control room to await a hospital tug. I was told by one of my fellow engineers that the air-start valve had blown up, that large pieces of it had been scattered around the engine room like shrapnel, and that one of these pieces must have hit me on the right knee.

Maybe it was the effect of Joe's rum, but I started to find that I just did not care about anything anymore, and I was beginning to feel numb all over. I started to try and figure out what would happen next, as they hauled me with a winch up the vertical conning tower hatch, over the bulging saddle tanks of the submarine and into a waiting launch, which was wallowing badly in a heavy sea. How the launch got there and from where it came, I just do not recall, and it felt like I had just floated out of the submarine conning tower and wafted gently over the side. The helpers then dumped me with little ado on the heaving deck of the launch and injected me with morphine. The launch was then quickly shoved off before leaving the smoking hull of *Osiris* behind.

It was then that I noticed a youngish-looking fellow in a somewhat weatherworn raincoat. He approached me with a friendly grin, dropped on one knee and asked, "What is it like down there?" Put yourself in my position, half slewed with Joe's "neaters" of rum, wrapped up like a sausage with something somewhere inside beginning to hurt like hell, and you might better understand why I replied, "down where?" "In the submarine," said the young fellow. Then he got all apologetic and explained, "I'm from *The Herald*. I want to get the story of what happened down there." At the moment, the only Herald of my acquaintance was a pretty fast destroyer which I knew was a good few thousand miles away in the China Seas, and I was just about to tell the young fellow he was a long way adrift from his ship when it dawned on me that I was being interviewed by a newspaper-man. Maybe it was Joe's rum again, but I just told that youngster exactly what it was like, and he said "Thank you very much" and stuck a cigarette into my face when he saw something was hurting me pretty badly again.

It did not take long for me to be transferred to a bed in Stonehouse Hospital, Portsmouth, where my leg was x-rayed, and it was explained to me that my whole knee joint had been shattered. I underwent an operation, and when I woke up I was not totally sure whether my leg had been amputated or not. With great apprehension I tried to wiggle my toes, and to my relief found that I could still feel them.

My knee joint had been removed though, which left me with a stiff right leg that was unable to be bent. Later, though, there were complications and my leg turned septic. The surgeon who had performed the operation, Lieutenant Keating, discussed with me the problems, and told me that I had septicaemia. I ran some very high temperatures, and I often had hallucinations. More operations followed, and at times I think there were doubts as to whether I would survive. Gradually my condition improved and eventually I was allowed to get out of bed, using a calliper around my leg, and crutches. I was at times allowed out, and I remember one of my first excursions was to see my first talking film, *The Thin Man* starring William Powell.

During my time in hospital I was, however, comforted by visits from a lady called Marie Guppy, who I had originally met on my travels with the navy out to Hong Kong. She had been working there as a Queen's Army schoolmistress in the British colony, but had recently returned to Britain, which meant she was able to visit me quite frequently. Gradually my condition improved, and eventually I was allowed to get out of bed more regularly, and was at last able to walk again without the use of callipers and the support of crutches.

CHAPTER TWO

A New Life

So my career in the navy came to an end, but a new part of my life was now about to begin. Marie and I fell in love, decided to marry, and went to live in Purley, South London. I got a job as an engineer at the large department store Harrods, looking after the engine rooms that supplied power to the store. Marie was a teacher at the Guard's Depot at Caterham, in Surrey, and we lived in lodgings that cost 30 shillings per week. I had to work shift hours at Harrods, which involved work at nights, and also sometimes on the weekends. As a result, Marie and I did not get to see as much of each other as we would have liked. Marie was aware that she would soon be due for another tour with the British Army, and thought that this was likely to be in India. She did not particularly want to go to India, and in order to get around this applied to go to Hong Kong instead.

She already knew Hong Kong, and liked it there, but the main question would be whether she could take me with her. After she put in her application for Hong Kong I was called for an interview at Caterham with Viscount Marsham. He was very pleasant and welcoming, and we had a long chat together about the possibility of me travelling out to Hong Kong with Marie. As far as he was concerned there would be no problem, and I made the necessary arrangements for my passage. The only condition was that I had to pay an indulgence passage fee of three shillings and sixpence per day.

We were due to leave on 9th October 1931. In the meantime we made preparations, including packing trunks, and for this my staff discount at Harrods came in very useful. We also had to transfer funds to accounts in Hong Kong, in advance of our arrival. The day of our departure finally arrived, and we were due to sail from Southampton on a troop ship called the *Neuralia*. On the quayside the band played "Good-Byee," as we waved goodbye to our families, and the ship then set off on a thirty-three day trip to Hong Kong. We left Southampton water behind, accompanied by RAF seaplanes that circled about us skimming the water and then circling overhead with a roar of engines.

The next day our ship was rolling horribly, and this went on for many hours. All the passengers were laid low, and as a result the dinning room was deserted. We had endured the aftermath of a severe storm, which caused a persistent roll in the sea. Eventually, though, the thick mist that covered the sea cleared, and we were abreast with Cape Ushant. The weather from then on improved, and everyone started to feel better. Marie became acquainted with her future colleagues at the Garrison School, who were also on board returning to Hong Kong. I felt rather strange being a civilian, and when people asked me what I was going to do, I had to reply that I didn't know.

We passed Cape Finnisterre and headed towards our first destination, Gibraltar. A battalion of the Royal Welch Fusiliers were due to disembark there to relieve The Lincolns, who were due to come with us to take up duties in Hong Kong. The Welch Fusiliers brought their mascot on board, a big pure white goat with widespread horns painted in gilt, and also a pack of beagle hounds that they exercised each morning on deck. It was a strange thing to hear the baying of a hound way out at sea.

On the fourth day of our trip we were abreast of the mouth of the River Tagus, and we could see Lisbon very clearly. We had earlier been able to see some whales, as well as "oilers" and cargo steamers. Ahead of us was Cape St Vincent, and I paused to remember the crew of the submarine K5, who sank there due to unknown causes in 1919. Our course took us past the coast of Spain, which was fringed with yellow sand. Dotted among the green of the hills could be discerned little white cottages that seemed so far from civilisation that I wondered whether anybody inhabited them.

On our fifth day we sighted the coast of Morocco, just before entering the Straights of Gibraltar. We came in sight of Gibraltar, and as we approached the quayside, soldiers were there to welcome us, and the ship soon became the scene of orderly disorder. We went ashore in Gibraltar for a little sightseeing and also to exercise, having been confined to the ship for the past five days. Gibraltar Dockyard seemed strangely empty, due no doubt to the fact that the Mediterranean fleet were away exercising at sea, which was their usual routine at this time of the year. We walked out of the dockyard where there was a very dusty road, and uninviting amenities. The dockyard quarters were very much like London tenement buildings, and very ugly. Soon, however, we passed The Alameda Gardens, which are very well arranged and laid out with trees and tropical plants. Naturally they did not look very pretty at that time of the year, but in the summer were no doubt a beautiful sight.

We then passed under a very old archway, dated 1558 and built by Charles VI of Spain, and went into Main Street. The full length of Main Street was full of so-called "curio shops," and as we passed them the proprietors of the shops stood on the pavement and tried to sell us their wares. We managed to find a tearoom to take some refreshment, and then returned to the ship. Nobody on board seemed to be very impressed by Gibraltar, and we were grateful when the *Neuralia* resumed its journey.

Our course then took us due east and we skirted the coast of Morocco. We became well acquainted with our fellow passengers while onboard, and the people from Hong Kong all seemed very nice and we hoped to make many friends in the colony. At nighttime The Lincolns sometimes prepared a dance on deck, which was illuminated with coloured lights and looked very pretty. On other nights a "sing-song" was arranged, which was fun for the passengers, but must have been a problem for the off-duty staff who were trying to sleep!

On the twelfth day of the voyage we arrived at Port Said. It was some time before the buildings on shore could be seen, and the first thing we saw was a monument erected to the memory of Ferdinand de Lesseps, the French engineer who planned and designed the construction of the Suez Canal, the most important waterway in the world. Passing the monument, we steamed parallel to the shore of Port Said harbour, along which were the various shipping company offices interspersed with restaurants and cafes. Eventually we arrived at The Suez Canal Company building, which was the most imposing building on the harbour. A little way past this building the *Neuralia* dropped anchor and in an incredibly short space of time we were surrounded by coal lighters, and crowded with natives whose bodies were covered with coal dust. The coaling ships in Port Said took a long time, occupying some five or six hours, and the whole process was carried out entirely by manual labour. The coal was carried on board in baskets and up steeply inclined planks leading to the ship's bunkers. In the harbour there were ships from all nations, including a motor vessel from Glasgow, and lying astern was a ship from Marseilles and then another from Russia.

We eventually got to shore and upon landing, we found our way to the Boulevard de Fouad, the main thoroughfare of Port Said. There were shops of all descriptions, from modish Paris milliners to the lowest dealer of oriental trash. The Boulevard ran the full length of the town, then led down to the seafront to which we walked and found a sandy beach, with bathing huts all reminiscent of Bognor Regis at home. The sand was fine and loose and unpleasant to walk upon, and was effectively the edge of the desert upon which Port Said is built. We then walked along the breakwater leading up to the de Lesseps Statue. It was a splendid bronze monument, with de Lesseps name surrounded in laurels, and a fitting tribute to the man who halved the distance from East to West. In the evening we made our way back through town, which was all lit up, and then back towards the dockyard and ship, which had almost finished coaling.

The following day our ship passed through the Suez Canal, and the desert could be seen on either side of the *Neuralia*, with the Arabian Desert on the port side and the Sahara on the other. In the early morning there was an icy cold breeze blowing over the sands, which seemed remarkable considering the fierce heat that the desert reached during the day. As we proceeded along the canal, the banks gradually grew higher, obscuring our view across the sandy wastes, until we reached a point called the "deepest-cut" where the embankment was 52 feet high. From deepest cut the banks gradually grew lower until there was an uninterrupted view across the desert on either side again, and in the far distance there were signs of habitation. An RAF aeroplane circled over our heads as we neared Ismailia, which was the first station on the canal.

The little quayside at Ismailia was pretty, and full of native crafts.

Around Ismailia the palm trees grew in profusion, and their green seemed to be the more luxuriant in contrast to the white glare of empty desert. The Egyptian Camel Corps combed the banks on the lookout for smugglers of hashish, and nearby was a famous landmark, the tomb of Sheikh Enedek, who was the deadly enemy of the people who constructed the canal. He resented this invasion of his territory, and the engineers were greatly hampered by his constant attacks on them, until finally a settlement was made and a truce called. Along the route of the canal, relics of the Great War could also be seen, and there were remains of entrenchments and barbed wire entanglements, and with a powerful telescope morbid skeletons could also be seen. It was the battlefront occupied by the Australians in the Great War when they successfully protected the canal, and from here Allenby had commenced his march onto Jerusalem, which was a tremendous undertaking.

From this point onwards the Sahara side grew more varying, while on the Arabian side there was an unaltered empty expanse of desert. On the Sahara side the little stations of The Suez Canal Company were more frequent, with the biggest and most important of these being El Pantara, El Gunerol and Suakim. There was also a memorial of curious design, which had been erected by the French on the Sahara side. The laying of foundations for this memorial, and transport of the great stone blocks used in its construction, was no mean undertaking and took five years to complete. It was, however, a magnificent and imposing tribute to the heroes of The Great War for civilisation, and looked most impressive and imposing in the desert setting.

We passed mighty dredgers at various intervals down the canal, which was constantly being dredged from end to end. On each one of these was a solitary white engineer in charge of a native gang. There was care and maintenance of the canal banks constantly taking place, and in places it had become necessary to sink concrete reinforcements. We were now in sight of Suez and Port Tewfik, which like most places looked very inviting when viewed from a ship, but I knew that these two particular places were ranked first among the most unsavoury spots in the area, with the sole purpose of being coaling stations.

We stopped a short while at Suez while the company's agent came aboard to arrange payment for our ship passing through the canal. I was not certain of the amount of the toll, but I was told that it extended well into four figures. The charge was made at so much per head on the number of passengers, and also in accordance with the ship's tonnage. It must have cost a mighty sum to allow *Neuralia* and her troops to traverse the seventy-odd miles of canal. During our short stop at Suez we had a beautiful view of the sun setting over the mighty Attaka Mountains. Somewhere in those mountains were the Wells of Moses, where according to biblical fable Moses was commanded by our Lord to strike the bare rock with his rod, whereupon water gushed forth. It is said that this water still runs, and has done so without a single lull right through the ages. It is also said that the water is always ice cold, and is sufficient to freeze a tin of fruit or a bottle of beer. Well done, Moses!

Our journey then took us onto the Red Sea where it started to get considerably hotter. The heat affected many passengers on board, and at nighttime the cabin was like a cauldron. The voyage through the Red Sea was the worst part of the whole journey, as it occupied the best part of four days, during which there was nothing in sight all around us but sea. However, one small item of interest to us was being able to see flying fish, and other passengers said they had seen sharks. After sixteen days of our voyage we left the Red Sea in our wake, and moved onto the cooler Indian Ocean. There was little else to see from onboard ship though, and it would take a further four days to reach our next destination, Colombo.

We eventually reached Colombo, and the troops gathered onboard ready to land for their first run ashore since Gibraltar. Colombo had an artificial harbour bounded by two breakwaters, similar to that of Gibraltar but much larger in size. The port was capable of accommodating a tremendous amount of shipping, and there were many classes there when we arrived. These included two blue funnel-lined boats, *The Atenor* and *Achilles*, and some *Bibby Line* boats, *The Worcestershire* and *Somersetshire*. There were also two ships of the H.M. Indian Marine, the *Fowey* and *Fox*, flying the white ensign of H.M. Navy.

As the ship got closer to the port it was surrounded by many smaller vessels as it had in Gibraltar. Among the earliest to board *Neuralia* were the Dhobi Wallahs, or in plainer language, the laundry men who are famous figures in Colombo. We commandeered one of these, and presented him with a large bundle of dirty washing which he promised to deliver at midnight. Nobody knows what mysterious methods these Dhobies resort to, but the fact remains that they will wash, starch and iron a whole pile of clothes in two or three hours, and return it completely dried and aired and perfectly laundered.

My first impression of landing in Colombo was not particularly good. It looked rather squalid from the landing jetty, with the usual crowd of insistent beggars and touts. We changed our money into native currency, receiving 13.5 Rupees for £1, and then wasted no time in getting clear of the jetty and into the town. We stopped at the Bristol Hotel for refreshment and afterwards took a rickshaw ride, with the rickshaw boy acting as a guide. "I like you see Cinnamon Gardens, you look see garden and then I take you Buddhist Temple, you can look there and then come back to city different way, I show you native town . . . very nice Sah!" All of which we agreed to, and so off we set at a good jog-trot. We saw the military barracks, and the army quarters that were very pleasantly situated and very clean, but did not pay a call because we had no acquaintances there at the present time.

Our road took us past a lot of recreation grounds belonging to various clubs. Cingalese people are very keen on all kinds of sport, and quite adept at Association Football. We saw several games in progress, the players being barefoot and dressed in coloured sarongs, and they could kick equally as well as a player at home who wears padded and studded boots. Most of the buildings we passed were tea factories, which was no surprise as tea planting and manufacturing was the staple industry of Ceylon. There were also many motor garages with the old familiar pumps, and advertising signs like the ones at home. We passed through a sort of residential street where the better class Europeans live, and where there were very attractive bungalows with pretty gardens. We stopped at the wall of one garden, and I was told by our rickshaw boy to stand on the seat of my rickshaw to pick a "temple flower for Lady." These temple flowers were a shaded pink blossom growing in clusters, and had a peculiarly sweet and seductive perfume. Eventually we arrived at the famous Cinnamon Gardens, where we dismounted from our rickshaws and went into the gardens. A guide took us in hand and showed us all over the gardens, but it is impossible for me remember the varied and wonderful things he showed us, except for many Rubber, Banyan, and Cinnamon Trees.

Dusk was falling, and we had doubts about visiting the Buddhist Temple, but our guide was determined to take us. Arriving at the temple, we again dismounted and entered a courtyard that looked very mysterious and alluring in the blue evening light. In the centre of the courtyard stood a huge dome in which was supposed to be the Buddha's spirit. Around this in the dark shadows one could distinguish the recumbent figures of worshippers lying prone. We were then led to the temple, where at the entrance we had to remove our shoes. Inside the temple we gazed in wonder at the recumbent figures of Buddha and all his relations. We laid flowers on the altar at the invitation of an old lady, who was paying her devotions. The walls were covered with crude illustrations of the life of Buddha, but it was a wonderful place. We then made our way to the Preaching Hall, where the Buddhist followers congregated daily to be exhorted by yellow-robbed priests.

It was soon time to leave and return to the ship. Upon reaching the jetty we dismissed our faithful steed with a payment amounting to about three shillings, which was small payment in truth for our man who carried us some seven miles or more in tropical heat. He explained that he had been forty years with his rickshaw, and did not find it hard work; he also said he could run seven miles at a stretch, and had four sons!

We set sail again, with another four days of our voyage until we were to reach our destination of Singapore. We were left with fond memories of Colombo, but life onboard the *Neuralia* during the remaining days was quite "hum-drum." We reached Singapore on 8th November and were greeted by monsoon weather, which prevented us from going ashore immediately. On 13th November we then reached Hong Kong, and were greeted by friends of Marie called the Freemans, who took us to our quarters in the barracks. Marie was made the Head School Mistress of the garrison school on Garden Road, which was on the lower part of the Hong Kong peak. She was given a quarter almost next to the school, and I set about making our accommodation comfortable.

I then needed to look for a job, and had envisaged that this would not prove to be too much of a problem. Among the many applications I made were enquiries to the Public Works Department, the Hong Kong Dockyards and British American Tobacco Company. However, I found that prospects were not much better in Hong Kong than they were back in

Britain, and instead of finding available vacancies I found that most organisations were making people redundant, with large number of Europeans out of work. I was then sent for by the Naval Hospital, as they were conducting a survey of all disabled servicemen in receipt of a pension. It seemed that the government was intent on cutting down expenses, and they were reviewing the circumstances of anybody in receipt of a disability pension. I had to go before a tribunal comprising various surgeons and officers, and they asked me questions about my circumstances. The upshot of this meeting was that my pension, which at that time was sixty-four pounds per year, was to be cut by ten percent, which was an experience that left me feeling very bitter.

Life in Hong Kong on the busy Queens Road Central,
as depicted in a postcard from the 1930's. *Author collection*

Our finances became a great anxiety to me, especially as Marie had told me that she was pregnant. In a desperate attempt to get a job, I put an advert in a local newspaper offering my services as a private tutor in English and Maths. To my surprise, the business became quite lucrative, and I became tutor to all kinds of people. One of the people that I taught English to was a businessman called Mr. Al Hoi Choi, who told me that he wanted to start a business in Hong Kong and asked me if I had any ideas. I suggested to him that there was an opening for an advertising agency, and that if he wanted to put up the money then I would have a go at running it for him. He liked this plan and rented an office, from which we then started what we rather grandly called "The International Advertising Service." One of our first projects was for a local cinema that wanted to improve the leaflets that they handed out advertising the films being shown. I thought that this could be developed into a magazine, which had pictures of the film stars as well as details about the films. We started producing the magazine, and in addition to information about the films, also managed to fill it with a variety of advertisements. The magazine proved to be a great success, but in spite of this, I was still looking for something better.

Hong Kong Island in the 1930's before the Japanese invasion, where Harold had a variety of jobs before becoming a newspaperman. *Author collection*

Marie was now heavily pregnant, and eventually gave birth to a baby girl in Victoria Hospital, who we named Patricia Marie. Now with my additional responsibilities, I intensified my search for a more permanent and secure job. Before long an opportunity arose when I was introduced one day to Mr. Miron Simon, the manager of an American firm of stockbrokers called Swan, Culbertson and Fritz. They were quite well established in Hong Kong, and worked mainly at night because of the time difference between Hong Kong and New York. The position that Mr. Simon wanted me to take up was handling telephone enquiries regarding trading on the stock markets.

So my working day now consisted of the following jobs: in the morning I was a private tutor; afternoon an advertising manager; evenings I was a stock broker's "contact man." There was also a Portuguese man working in the stockbroker office, and a Chinese man called Mr. Yip. I found the stockbroker job to be very interesting. I processed transactions via telephone or cable on the New York stock exchange, and informed customers of the price at which shares had been bought and sold. The job also put me in contact with some very wealthy people whose transactions would quite often involve tens of thousands of pounds, especially if they were dealing in commodities. It also gave me an insight into how the world of finance worked, at a time when there were a lot of countries coming out of financial depression.

I was less concerned over work and my prospects now, and I thought that the position with the stockbroker was something I could continue with when we returned to Britain. Everything seemed to be going well, and we even decided to buy our first car. One of the main reasons for wanting a car was that we liked to go and visit an area in the south of Hong Kong called Repulse Bay. It was a beautiful setting, where we owned a bamboo beach hut known as a *matshed*. It would have been possible to get there by bus, but it was awkward when we had all our things to carry and a small baby. I needed to learn to drive a car, and in 1933 Hong Kong you were required to take a driving test, even though this had not yet been introduced to the United Kingdom. On my first attempt I failed, but was very pleased when I managed to pass the second time around. Driving in Hong Kong was not that easy, as it is a peak 1,400 feet high, and most of the roads were steep, narrow, and winding. We used to load the car up with a picnic, and go over to Repulse Bay and the New Territories at every available opportunity.

I was becoming more interested in the stockbroker business, and the factors that made the market fluctuate. At this time the British Government was trying to raise money by issuing bonds. The American stockbrokers found these difficult to understand, and gave me the responsibility to find out more about them. I went to interview various bank managers and financiers to get information about the bonds, and then started dealing with all enquiries and transactions relating to them back in the office. As a result, my profile within the business increased, and my efforts in dealing with these English bonds helped to increase business for the brokers. Once more my interest in how the stock market fluctuated grew, and I thought that it would be a good idea if we recorded them in a chart or graph and published it in a newsletter that we could give to our clients.

I suggested this to Mr. Simon, and he was very much in favour of the idea. On reflection, this was one of the most audacious things that I had ever done in my life: here I was, an ex-naval engineer, with relatively little experience of the financial world, commenting on the fluctuations that took place on the New York Stock Exchange. I began producing the newsletter on Sunday evenings, using just pen and paper. I would then present my work to Mr. Simon for approval, and then the newsletter would be printed and sent to bankers, brokers, and businesses. The newsletter was a big success, and it seemed to me quite incredible that I was writing about the world of finance, and that my findings were not only being accepted, but also praised.

The newsletter also attracted the attention of *The South China Morning Post*, whose editor came to visit Swan, Culbertson and Fritz, and asked

whether it would be possible to reproduce the newsletter in their paper. Mr. Simon was more than happy for this to happen, as it would provide good publicity for the firm. So the newsletter appeared as a regular feature in the paper, receiving a great deal of attention from many people including John Morris, who was the Far Eastern Manager of the United Press Associ-

Marie and Pat outside their bamboo matshed in Repulse Bay, Hong Kong. *Author collection*

ation. He wrote to our firm and asked if I could do some work for the United Press. Mr. Simon told me about the inquiry, and I was very keen to give it a go, as I could see that further career prospects might stem from it. John Morris then came to our offices to meet me, and explained that the United Press was a news agency that collected news from all over the world and at that time they were particularly interested in financial news. To my surprise, he asked me if I would open a United Press office in Hong Kong. This obviously came as a bit of a shock to me. His proposal was more substantial than I had anticipated and I needed to make a decision over what to do, because Marie was due to go back to Britain. It was now 1934 and she had finished her three-year tour of duty. I felt that there would be more opportunities for me in the future if I started working for United Press, rather than just pursuing the work of a stockbroker. In the end we decided that Marie would return home with Patricia, and I would stay in Hong Kong.

John Morris did not stay too long in Hong Kong, and I was left to get the United Press office established by myself. I approached Ben Wylie, General Manager of *The South China Morning Post*, with whom I had had some dealings while working for the advertising agency, to get advice and also to see if he would let me have an office within his premises. He agreed

Repulse Bay, Hong Kong, the scene of many happy times for Harold, Marie and Pat before the Japanese invasion in 1941. *Author collection*

to let me have a desk in their newsroom, so I purchased various pieces of equipment including a typewriter, mimeograph machine, and stencils for duplicating news bulletins. I had hardly used a typewriter before, and spent many hours practising, mainly with two fingers, trying to increase my speed. I also spent some time visiting other newspapers in Hong Kong to introduce the services that could be provided by the United Press.

In January 1935 the office was ready to start operating. My first assignment was posted to me from New York, which was to report on the imminent birth of a baby to the wife of the American Council General, Mrs. Helen Spiker, who was also a famous socialite. The United Press was keen to report on the birth. Even though it was not the type of news story they would normally cover, they were hoping to become a client of *The Washington Post* and wanted to impress them with the speed of their service. Mrs. Spiker lived in Canton, which was over 100 miles away from Hong Kong and too far for me to travel from the office to report on the story. So I got in contact with the midwife who was looking after Mrs. Spiker, and asked her if she would call me as soon as the baby was born and give me the details. The midwife kept her word and phoned in the early hours of the morning after the birth. I then got immediately on the phone to the cable office and dictated my first news story:

Helen. Wife of C.J. Spiker American Council General.
Gave birth to baby son 7lb both well.

I felt confident that I had been first with the story, and was quite pleased with my work. Two weeks later I got a letter from United Press in New York, which said that I would be gratified to know that I was five days ahead of our opposition, Reuters and The Associated Press, with releasing the story. However, they also told me that my cable was too long, and as a result cost far too much. They suggested that my cable could have been shortened. First, by not naming the American Council General's wife or stating to whom she was married, as they had already informed me of these facts. They also said that there was no need to describe the event as a birth of a baby, which was self-explanatory. If Mrs. Spiker had given birth to a 21-year-old son, that would have been news! They suggested that the cable could have read . . . Spiker birthed son. This was my first lesson in what was known in the newspaper world as *cabelese*.

The United Press also wanted me to get a radio transmitting service set up, so that we did not have to rely on communicating just by cable, which was something that added to their costs. There was, however, a problem with establishing a reception for radio transmission, because Hong Kong was surrounded by hills. It would have been better if maybe the radio station was established at the top of the peak, but this was quite a long way out of the city and was inconvenient. I had an idea, though, as to how this problem could be overcome: if there was a radio station outside of Hong Kong, then signals from it could be received there and then transmitted onto us. I researched this possibility, and found a station that was based in Macao, which is a small peninsula 30 miles south of Hong Kong under Portuguese ownership. I met with the Post Master General there, a Señor Martin, who was a very jolly man with a weakness for wine and gambling.

At first he only seemed interested in these latter activities, and it took me two days of drinking wine and playing *fan-tan*, a game using bamboo sticks, before we eventually got round to talking about the radio transmission. However, an arrangement was eventually established where radio transmissions would be received in Macao, and then transmitted onto Hong Kong via the telephone system. To my surprise, I also found that every month Señor Martin would send me a cheque for $1,200. I later found out that this was because the news that was being received in Macao was of great use to him, as it contained details regarding the commodities markets in advance of everyone else, which he could then use to his advantage.

Eventually though, we were able to establish our own radio station, and an engineer called George Baxter, who was an expert in radio transmission, erected an aerial on top of the building housing *The South China Morning Post*. He was also able to copy the news via Morse code at a rate of 72 words per minute, so that we had up-to-date news at our fingertips. The radio station really helped to establish the United Press office, because it put us way ahead of our rivals with the news. Financial news was of particular interest to many bankers and businessmen in Hong Kong, the importance of which was increased as President Roosevelt began making changes to the American economy.

My work at the newspaper also brought me into contact with many interesting and famous people who visited Hong Kong. These included:

playwright and composer Noel Coward; famous actors such as Douglas Fairbanks Senior and Carol Lombard; and playwright and author George Bernard Shaw. One of the most memorable persons I met, however, was Charlie Chaplin, who came to Hong Kong when his film *Modern Times* was released. I was shocked when I received a cable from New York, stating that there had been reports that Charlie Chaplin had died in the Far East, and asking if I knew anything about the story. I investigated this, and found out that Charlie Chaplin had already left Hong Kong and gone to Indo-China. So I sent Chaplin a telegram simply saying "Are you dead? If not please reply to this telegram." Eventually I got a most amusing reply from him saying "No! Not yet! Are you?" Charlie Chaplin later returned to Hong Kong, and I had the opportunity to speak to him again at a party. I remember saying to him that Hitler had copied his style of moustache, and he agreed and said jokingly that he should do something about it. In subsequent years I have often wondered whether this conversation may have started his inspiration for the film *The Great Dictator*.

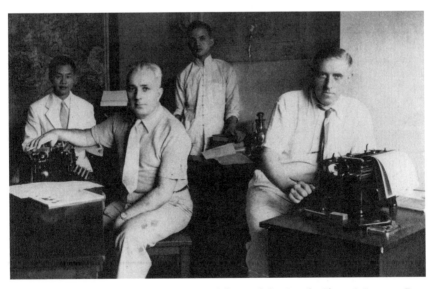

The Hong Kong UP Bureau on the 2nd floor of the South China Morning Post Building in 1937. From right to left: George Baxter, Hung Chiu (office assistant), Harold Guard and Lai Shau-shek (overnight editor). Lai became a correspondent for Ta-Kung-Pao, one of the largest newspapers in China after the Second World War. *Author collection*

CHAPTER THREE

Pre-War Hong Kong

I n 1936 there was a great deal of unrest in the world. Italy had invaded
Ethiopia and Hitler had come to power in Germany. There was civil
war in Spain as well as unrest in China and Japan, and as a result our
office was extremely busy managing all the news as it came in about these
events. In Hong Kong at this time there were many different nationalities,
including Germans, Japanese, and Chinese, and I was approached by an
inspector from the Special Branch, called Shannon, who asked me to pass
on any information that may come my way about these various factions
that I thought might be suspicious. With my newspaper connections I was
able to go into the German Club in Hong Kong, and mingle amongst its
members in order to build up a dossier on people who may be Nazi sym-
pathisers. One of these people was a man called Martin Hesse, who apparently was the brother of Rudolph Hesse, Hitler's deputy. I also observed
the Japanese community and helped identify an influential spy called
Ohura. He was a Japanese colonel posing as a civilian, and monitoring
things such as military installations and water supplies, which would be of
help in the event of a military invasion.

President Roosevelt's new monetary policies were having a great effect
on the business markets in Hong Kong. Normally the dollar at this time

was worth two shillings, but it would fluctuate and sometimes go as high as three shillings, and then as low as eleven pence. Eventually the government decided to act, and they called a meeting of the "Big Five Banks," which included The Hong Kong and Shanghai Bank, The Bank of China, The First National City Bank, The Chartered Bank and The Mercantile Bank, although they did not invite The Chase Bank. The vice president of The Chase Bank was David Bigger, who was very upset about not being included in the Big Five. I met with him, and he was very disparaging about the Big Five and told me that he knew already what they were going to discuss. He told me that the government was going to withdraw all the silver dollars and issue a paper currency, that the currency would be printed by Walter Lowe and Company in Britain, and that it would be brought out to Hong Kong on a P&O ship called the *Royal Pindy* and arrive sometime in October. He also added that the value of the dollar would be fixed at one shilling and three pence, and that I could print everything he had told me as long as I did not reveal the source.

So I printed the story that the value of the Hong Kong dollar was going to be fixed at one shilling and three pence, and that the Chinese silver dollar was going to be withdrawn. This story created a lot of unrest, as the value of some people's sterling holdings in Hong Kong would be halved. The chairman of the Big Five Banks immediately denied that the story was true, and I came under a great deal of pressure to either retract the story or reveal my source of information. David Bigger told me to stick to the story, because he said that in the end it would turn out to be true. Weeks and months went by before the silver dollar was eventually withdrawn, and the price of the new paper-based currency was fixed. It was of great relief to me, as I thought that I might get fired over the incident.

The other very big story in 1936 was the story of King Edward VIII, who had succeeded King George V, and had had an affair with an American woman named Mrs. Simpson. These happenings had not been reported in the British press at all, and there had been nothing in the Reuters news about it, but because the United Press was an American news agency they had reports on the whole affair. In fact, the story was first broken by a United Press reporter named Tosty Russell, who had found out that Mrs. Simpson was being divorced from her husband in a small town in Suffolk, England called Ipswich. The story was printed in *The*

South China Morning Post and caused a great deal of controversy, and many people were critical of me and the United Press for revealing it. Finally the abdication of King Edward VIII took place and the United Press was vindicated—its reputation was enhanced and business was increased in the office. The manager of *The South China Morning Post*, a Scotsman called Ben Wylie, saw the potential of the United Press services, and asked me if our services could be made exclusive to him. I agreed to do this, providing that the subscription fee was increased by five pounds.

I was now becoming well established within the newspaper industry in Hong Kong, and one day was asked by Ben Wylie, the general manager of the *Hong Kong Telegraph*, if I would temporarily manage his newspaper for him. Ben was a good client of ours; at the time he had a staff shortage because of an employee that had been sent home to England for a serious surgical operation. I agreed to the arrangement while also continuing with my existing job at the United Press, who at that time were selling what they called a "feature service" to newspapers. So, as the manager of the United Press, I wrote to the manager of the *Hong Kong Telegraph*, which was myself, with the proposition of the "feature service." Then, as the manager of the *Hong Kong Telegraph*, I wrote a letter back to the manager of the United Press office, arranging a meeting with myself. Then to clinch the deal I had to go to Ben Wylie, the general manager of the *Hong Kong Telegraph*, to get his approval. I told him that I had received a letter from the United Press office in Hong Kong, offering a "feature service" for the newspaper, and that I thought that it seemed like a good idea. He asked if I had managed to negotiate the price down with the United Press, and I said that I had made a good arrangement, and then comically the deal went through.

I did at times, though, get disillusioned with the autocracy of government, and the attitudes of society in Hong Kong. So in order to poke fun, I created a character called Herbert Higgs, who had a weekly column in the *Hong Kong Telegraph*. His column was headed, "Herbert Higgs in His Own Write." The editor told me later that the Herbert Higgs column actually put the sales up, and that it was very popular. Herbert Higgs's popularity was lasting, and I was asked again to write under the pseudo name in 1953, when I was more complementary, saying how safe it felt now in Hong Kong. This story got splashed on the front page of the *Hong*

Kong Telegraph and the next day the whole of the edition had sold out. As a result, the Governor of Hong Kong, Sir Mark Young, sent for me, and received me very well, thanking me for writing the column.

Another news item that I investigated was the drugs trade in Hong Kong. My interest in this had been prompted through an American friend called Arthur Campbell, who was an official at the United States Treasury, appointed to the Far East as part of the anti-narcotics team. He was a very jolly companion, but also a very astute and clever detective. Through him I managed to get a deep insight into the trade of drugs, and wrote a number of stories about it. I remember that there was a famous biscuit manufacturer in Hong Kong who made a thin wafer-like biscuit that was sold in very attractive decorated tins. These were exported to the USA, and through Arthur Campbell's investigations it was revealed that some of the tins contained cocaine. This was worth a great deal of money, because at that time cocaine was selling at $700 per ounce in the USA. There was another firm that was exporting linen blankets to San Francisco. It was discovered by the narcotics team that when the blankets reached their destination, they were taken away and boiled, and the distilled water was found to contain huge amounts of cocaine. The drug trade itself built up a countertrade, where informers on the drug trade received huge rewards, and if a seizure was made in a drugs raid they would get a third of the value of the haul. It was very interesting for me to see how the criminal fraternity operated in Hong Kong.

At the end of 1936 I was starting to feel very homesick, and had been getting letters from Marie, in which it was apparent that she was also feeling unhappy. She had been mourning the death of her brother, but she was also feeling very lonely, and asked whether it would be possible for me to come home and join her for a while. I was very much in favour of this, as it had been six years since I'd had a holiday, and during that time I had been working very hard to establish myself in a new career. So I wrote to John Morris and asked if I could have leave of absence, to see if I could go home and comfort Marie. At the beginning of 1937 John Morris wrote to me and said that providing I could make arrangements in Hong Kong to cover the operations of the United Press office, then I could have my leave of absence. I talked it over with John Shaw, the editor of the *Hong Kong Telegraph*, whose wife was also going on leave, and it was arranged that he would stay in the flat while I was away. I then employed a temporary member of staff to help in the office, a young Englishman named Les Pearson, who would work with George Baxter.

So I could now start making arrangements for coming home, and had thought of plans to travel in a rather spectacular manner. One of these was to come home on the Trans Siberian Express. It would have taken me from Hong Kong to London in about twenty-one days, but proved to be a very laborious business, because there were so many visas that were needed for the journey. The other more ambitious plan was to fly home on an airmail postage plane. At that time there was an airline called Imperial Airways that flew mail only from London to Hong Kong. It used to take about a week if weather conditions were good, but sometimes you were able to get a letter in five days. I hit upon the idea of getting myself on the plane, but as an item of mail. I asked Imperial Airways about this, and to my surprise they were very enthusiastic. The plan was to wear a leather coat that would be covered in postage stamps, which would cover the cost of my delivery. The main condition was that I would not be able to leave the plane at all, and would be treated strictly as mail. This presented a problem regarding feeding, though The Horlicks Company, who made malted milk, were interested in sponsoring me by giving me a supply of their tablets that would keep me going for the seven-day trip. The project seemed to be all set until somebody spoilt it by discovering that livestock could not be carried by the Royal Mail. Eventually though, I managed to book myself a passage on one of the Japanese *NYK Lines*, as they were the cheapest available. In April 1937 I finally embarked on my trip home, and I made up my mind that whilst on board I was going to rest. It was actually a very pleasant time on board, but I was glad when I finally arrived home.

When I returned to Hong Kong the war in China was intensifying— the Japanese had invaded the Chinese mainland and were sweeping through it quite rapidly. They had captured Chunking and Nanking, and were coming swiftly southwards. We were receiving terrible stories from our United Press reporters in the field; Hong Kong had now become a sort of clearing centre for all the news and I was getting run off my feet. I had to hire more assistance, as we were keeping a 24-hour watch because things were happening so quickly in China. The only happy piece of news that came during this period was a letter from Marie saying that she was setting sail for Hong Kong in December, and that she should arrive sometime in the New Year.

During this time I also had a very intriguing call from my correspondent in Macao whose name was John Brager. He was such a dependable correspondent that for him to call me and ask me to go down there made me realise that something exciting was happening. So I went down as soon as I could, and he explained to me that there had arrived in the colony a Baron Ernst von Rusmunsen.*

The background of this Baron was that he had, until recently, been one of Hitler's top men, and had ranked about number five in the German hierarchy. He had then fallen out with Hitler because he did not agree with Hitler's plan for the invasion of Poland. As a result he had gone to China, where he had hoped to ingratiate himself with Chiang Kai-shek, who around that time was hiring a lot of German military advisors in his war against Japan. Baron Ernst Von Rusmunsen had failed to get along with Chiang Kai-shek, and in no time at all found himself short of money. He was now in Macao, and wanted to sell his story to the newspapers.

I met with the Baron in what seemed to me to be somewhat amusing circumstances. I was put into a big motorcar with curtains drawn down so I could not see where we were going, and we then drove for quite a long way. Macao's total area is only five square miles, so we must have driven for quite a long time in circles in order to confuse me, but we eventually arrived at a house, and in it was a man who could be described as looking similar to Lord Montgomery. The Baron was a slight moustached figure with a military bearing, and not at all the big German Nazi bully that I had envisaged in my mind. He had a lot of very interesting things to tell me about Hitler's plans for the invasion of Poland, then of France, and then ultimately the British Isles.

A lot of these ideas sounded rather fanciful, but what impressed me most of all was some blueprints he had of a glider that he said could carry up to fifty troops, and be launched across the channel. I was sufficiently well versed in reading blueprints to know that these things were genuine. He also had a blueprint for a pilot-less aircraft that would be propelled by

---

*Baron Ernst von Rusmunsen is the closest interpretation that can be made from the original tapes, and further research has failed to verify any other spelling of the name.

a rocket, and I was convinced that the intention was to use this rocket as a missile.

All the things he had told me seemed to be genuine, as we had plenty of evidence from all our dispatches that Hitler was determined to wage war. I returned to Hong Kong, and I sent a message to New York giving a very detailed account of what Baron Ernst Von Rusmunsen wanted to sell to us. The Baron wanted $50,000 as a down payment, and then a percentage of any of the syndication rights for his information. A very quick reply came back from the United Press in New York, which simply said, "Tell your Baron, go smoke another pipe!" I was very much surprised by this attitude, as the story appeared to be genuine and of great significance. Despite the setback, I thought that the Baron's information might be of interest to somebody else, so I went to see the contacts I had in Hong Kong who were connected with British Intelligence, but they thought the stories were fanciful and showed no interest at all. Shortly after that a man from *Colliers Magazine* came to Hong Kong, whose name was Jim Marshall. I told him the story of Baron Ernst Von Rusmunsen, and he went immediately off to Macao to see if he could find the Baron, but was unable to do so. That was a chapter closed as far as I was concerned, and I never heard anything more about it.

Another thing that happened around this time was the arrival of the "O-Class" submarines to Hong Kong. I took the opportunity to meet up with a lot of old shipmates of mine, and they had a very interesting story to tell me. They said that the "O-boats" were laid up with engine trouble and that there had been a very thorough enquiry into the cause of this; it had been established that the lubricating oil with which they had been served in the naval dockyard had not been a mineral oil at all, but a vegetable oil. This had caused a lot of problems in the engine, and the bearings and pistons had been badly scored. There was a theory amongst the crew that this had been an act of sabotage, and a court of enquiry had been set up to investigate the matter.

Later in 1939 another most interesting story came my way, from a British naval lieutenant called Richardson, who was on a light cruiser called the HMS *Dorsetshire*. Neither America nor Japan was in the war with Britain at the time, and yet this British cruiser had intercepted a Japanese liner, which I think was called the *Tatsuta Maru*, on the seas between San

Francisco and Yokohama. In mid-ocean they had put aboard a boarding party, and had promptly arrested 60 American citizens. They then brought them aboard HMS *Dorsetshire*, and taken them down to Hong Kong where they were put into Stanley Jail.

I have it on good authority that those American citizens were of German extraction, employed by the Standard Oil Company of California, and had been part of a very well organised sabotage ring against the Allies. It was the Standard Oil Company of California that had been responsible for delivering the lubricating oil to the naval dockyard in Hong Kong, and it was this lubricating oil that had put the six "O" class submarines out of action. The German-Americans working in the Standard Oil Company had got wind that naval intelligence were on their tracks, and had then tried to escape to Japan. Lieutenant Richardson, who had actually intercepted the Japanese cruiser, had pictures of the incident, but I could not use them in any way because I would have been prevented by the Official Secrets Act and censorship. To this day I do not know whether any official news was released about this incident, but it was most remarkable, and indicated to me how much subversive activity there was in Hong Kong at this time.

For me, 1938 started in a much happier way, when Marie and Patricia arrived back in Hong Kong, and I was overjoyed to be reunited with them. We now lived in a spacious well-appointed 2nd floor military flat on Hankow Road. Life, though, was getting more and more hectic, as the war around the world was escalating and news about it was flooding in day after day. By the middle of 1938 the Japanese had landed in a place called Bias Bay, which was not far from Hong Kong—they had confounded all the military pundits and charged across the great Chinese province of Canton. They captured Canton, and from there they spread out right along the Hong Kong border. More than once I went out to the border, and was able to look across and actually see the Chinese sentries with their bayonets fixed, standing under the Japanese flag glowering straight back at us. Back in Hong Kong a German cruiser, *The Gneisenau*, had sailed into the harbour to be used as a voting station. It was anchored for 48 hours, and all the Germans living in Hong Kong went aboard to cast their votes. It became apparent to me that a lot of them, who were long-term residents, were simply going to vote upon this German warship because they were frightened, and had been pressured into doing it. This was another indication to me that Hitler was busy putting his plans into place.

We frequently would meet quite a famous and legendary character in Hong Kong at that time, known as General "Two-Gun" Cohen. He was Jewish, and born in Manchester. His real name was Maurice Cohen, and somehow or other had gained a reputation for being a "tough guy." He had been a gunman in Canada, and I think perhaps his activities had made him a wanted man, and so he ended up in China on the run. I am not quite sure how it happened, but he became a close confidant of Doctor Sun Yat-Sen, who was the leader of the first Chinese rebellion against the old Imperialist rule in about 1911. Maurice Cohen had become a kind of bodyguard to Doctor Sun Yat-Sen, and a legend had grown up around him that he always carried two guns, hence his title "Two-Gun" Cohen. Maurice Cohen became very fond of Patricia, and at times we would meet with him in the Hong Kong Hotel, which was not far away from *The South Morning Post* building. He would frequently take Patricia off somewhere, after which she would return with a huge box of chocolates. In fact, Two-Gun Cohen, in spite of all the terrifying stories about him, was a very simple and kindly type of character.

In Hong Kong at the beginning of 1939 life was quite pleasant, and we used to go out to Repulse Bay where we had our bathing hut. The routine in the office was now at a workable level, and the pressures on me were decreasing. However, the menace of the Japanese was very real, and I was convinced that the only thing that stood in the way of a Japanese invasion in 1939 was that Germany and Russia had signed a non-aggression pact. The news from Europe, though, was ominous, as we heard about Hitler's invasion of Poland. The investigation that Inspector Shannon had done in identifying key German figures in Hong Kong had suddenly come into effect, and the suspects were immediately rounded up and placed straight into jail. The big question now was what would the Japanese do? It was a very menacing time, and I think that everyone in Hong Kong felt the pressure.

Things were very busy in the United Press office, and I found that the only way of coping with this was by drinking heavily. This upset Marie a lot, and didn't really like the person who I was becoming. I think it was a stroke of luck that I then had an accident which led to the end of this habit.

My friend Arthur Campbell, with whom I had covered a lot of stories in the drug trade, invited myself and Marie out one evening to a party. It was a strange party. Though there were not many people we knew, it was still a very nice party. When we came out of the house where the party was being held, it was very dark, and there were some shallow steps to walk down. Nearing the bottom of these steps, and in the darkness, I stumbled and fell, and felt my stiff leg crack. I knew it was broken. This was a frightening thing for me because I knew how frail the leg was, but fortunately we were not far from the naval hospital.

We had a group of people with us, and I asked them to get one of the sedan chairs and take me to the naval hospital. It was an agonising experience, because the sedan chairs tend to bounce up and down when they are being carried, so I was glad when the chair was set down outside the hospital and the duty surgeon came out to see me. They gave me a shot of morphine to take away the pain, got me set down for the night, and Marie then went home. In the morning she came back, and I was taken away for an x-ray—it was confirmed that the leg was broken, and it would need an operation to put it right again. So there I was back again in a naval hospital.

The operation was performed for no given reason under just a local anesthetic around the knee, with the intention of putting some pins through it. I was propped up on the operating table and could see everything that went on. The surgeon got a drill, and drilled a hole straight through my leg where the knee joint used to be. To my surprise this was quite painless. The surgeon then put some wires through my leg, and a plaster cast was placed around it from my ankle to my hip. I was then put back in bed, where I stayed for about three weeks before being allowed back home.

I had to spend about three months in the plaster, which seemed to be very thick. This proved to be quite a difficulty living in a second floor flat, but Marie made a seating pad for me, and when I wanted to go down the stairs, I did it on my backside. The weeks in that plaster were rather annoying, and difficult. Eventually I was called back to the hospital to have it removed. It was, however, a turning point that taught me a lesson about the heavy drinking, and getting things into perspective.

Christmas 1939 was very happy for us, but as it transpired it was to be the last one that we would spend in Hong Kong. International politics had taken many unexpected turns. Germany and Russia had formed a non-aggression pact, and this seemed to upset any plans Japan had for joining in the general offensive against Britain. Their troops were still stationed on the Hong Kong border and there was no doubt that they posed a massive threat, which made the Hong Kong government very uneasy. As a result it was decided to form an additional defence force in Hong Kong, and all British males of eighteen years and over were to be conscripted.

They wanted to set things up very quickly, and decided to organise a mass medical inspection of all eligible males, and this included me. The garrison school was taken over for a day, where about a dozen doctors congregated, and all the men had to pass between these doctors very quickly to be inspected. We all had to strip off down to our socks and shoes, and each of the doctors we passed before had a delegated task. One would look at your ears, another would sound your chest, and they gave all the men a very thorough check over. The comical part, though, was that I managed to go past all these doctors, and not one of them noticed that I had a stiff leg—so I passed fit for the Hong Kong defence corps! What they planned exactly to do with me I don't know, but I cannot think I would have been of much use to them.

In July 1940 the decision was taken to evacuate women and children from Hong Kong, except for those women who were performing what was called "essential services." The army wives and children had to go, and this included Marie and Pat. So one dreadful afternoon they boarded one of the *Empress* boats, which were boats that had been stripped of all their amenities so that they could be used to carry troops. They were embarked onboard very quickly, and set off for the Philippines, with a stop at Australia. It was not until I got back home that night that I suddenly felt a great emptiness. I was, however, able to move in with a friend, Bill Hirst, which helped ease my loss.

The situation in Hong Kong was now getting very worrying, and I started to make my own plans for getting out. As things turned out it was not necessary, because I had a message late in November from John Morris in Shanghai instructing me to pack up everything in Hong Kong and move down to Singapore. The United Press wanted to open an office there, and they wanted me to set it up. So I said goodbye to Bill Hirst, and left George Baxter to take over the office in Hong Kong, before sailing off to Singapore on a ship called the *President Jackson*. The trip was not that pleasant because there was a strike by the staff on board, but I arrived in Singapore safely and booked into the Raffles Hotel.

CHAPTER FOUR

Singapore Defence

E stablishing a news agency office anywhere is not an easy business, and is made even more difficult during wartime. Radio contacts needed setting up, along with other equipment like a teleprinter. I managed to find an office on Battery Road near the general post office to base our operation, and recruited some local people for staff. Chief amongst these was a man called Wee Kim Wee, who was a Straits-born Chinese, and had been Malaya's champion badminton player. He was very bright and dependable, and later in his life became President of Singapore. I also recruited another Malay man who was a very proficient teleprinter operator, whose name was Arshad. When our little office got underway, the news started coming in very quickly, but we managed to cope with the demands and got the United Press news service up and running.

One of the first people who I interviewed in Singapore was an old navy commander who had previously been in charge of an H-boat. His name was Admiral Sir Geoffrey Layton, and he had an office at the naval base. After I had finished my interview with him, he invited me back to his house for an, "off-the-record" chat. We went there in an official car, and I always remember the way he strode up to the veranda at the front of his house and sank down into a chair. Sir Geoffrey Layton then stripped off various parts of his uniform with some apparent relief, and declared; "Now I'm a bloody civvy too!" He then gave me a very honest and enlightening account of what he thought about the situation regarding the naval defences in Singapore. The main point that he made was that the island had twenty-six square miles of deep-sea anchorage offshore, which was large enough to take the whole of the British and American fleets, along with a dry-dock and workshops onshore. The only thing that was missing was a navy! It did seem incredible that although Singapore had such an extensive naval defensive facility, there were so few ships to form a fleet.

Pre-war Singapore. *Author collection*

As our news service became increasingly busy, John Morris decided to send me an assistant, whose name was Darrell Berrigan. He was a young American who had done a great deal of work for the United Press on the Chinese war front, as well as Indo-China. One of the earliest stories that we had to cover was the arrival of Australian troops onboard the *Queen Mary*. They were quickly disembarked at the naval base in Singapore, and shipped away "up country" into Malaya, to an area on the west coast known as Mersing. Now that I had an additional member of staff, I took advantage of the situation and travelled up into the Malay Peninsula to find out what conditions were like for the troops.

I was not able to cover the whole of the peninsula in my travels, as it is actually quite a large area. There were also a limited number of roads and railways that could be used, with quite a lot of the land being covered in thick vegetation. From a military point of view the density of the jungle was a good thing, as it meant that observations of the ground from aircraft were limited and would provide protection for any foot soldiers. The jungle could, though, also be inhospitable, with the protective canopy making conditions underneath it very hot and damp, which was not conducive to a lot of physical activity and made you feel very uncomfortable.

Despite this there was a great deal of commercial activity in and around the rubber plantations, and it was near the plantations where it was easiest to find a road or railway. Occasionally it was also possible to find a road

Singapore waterfront before the war, a hive of marine activity. *The Sydney Sun*

that went out to a coastal port—where the jungle became less dense, movement was less prohibitive. I was also told that there were more open areas of land in the north of the peninsula where there were rice fields, although moving from the west to east coasts could be hampered by a range of hills that pretty much ran all the way down it's length.

On my first visit to the Mersing area on the west coast, where the Australians had been sent, I found the troops to be in a very disgruntled mood. Despite there being some sandy stretches of beach on the west side, there were also some very unpleasant mangrove swamps. Their mood had not been made any better by reports coming from the Middle East, where their comrades were having some notable successes and covering themselves in glory. The Australians stationed in Malaya seemed unsure as to what they were doing there, and were almost in a militant mood when I spoke to them. I then went further up country where the Indian regiment was taking part in exercises. This visit proved to be most enlightening in regards to the benefit of the Malayan jungle as a natural defence for Singapore Island.

Officials wait at the Singapore dock to greet Australian troops. From the right in the foreground is Admiral Geoffrey Layton (wearing white) and Sir Shenton Thomas, Governor of Malaya. Troops were quickly dispatched and sent up into the Malay peninsula. *Newspaper unknown*

One of the officers commanding a regiment had previously been told that the section that he was responsible for was easy to defend because it was well protected by jungle. He had felt sceptical about these claims and decided to conduct an experiment, by taking some of his men along a road to a point where the jungle appeared to be at its thickest. He chose an objective point that was eight miles in the distance, and gave his men the order to make their way towards it. They managed to reach the destination within a few hours, and even though the jungle appeared at first to be dense in places, the undergrowth in some areas was composed just of saplings and shrubs, which could be cut down quite easily with a jungle knife. The giant trees of the tropical forest also were found at times to grow at intervals wide enough to make it possible to cut a path between their trunks. Staff officers came and inspected the area, and watched the Indians cut their way through the jungle. As a result, the defence scheme for that area was changed and applied to other areas as well. I witnessed this myself and was convinced that if the Japanese were to attack, they would be able to approach from the north and make their way easily through what was previously thought to be impenetrable jungle.

I also visited some Royal Air Force stations to find out what type of aircraft they had, and found that they mostly had two small airplanes, one called a Vildebeast and the other a Brewster Buffalo. These planes' top cruising speeds was about ninety miles per hour, and the Air Force ground staff were not too pleased, as they felt that the quantity of planes in their squadron was not big enough. My first trip up country had given me a very good insight as to the state of preparedness of the defences, which in addition to the comments made to me about the navy by Admiral Sir Geoffrey Layton, seemed to present quite a worrying situation.

When I got back to Singapore I immediately started to write a report on what I had found out. I can remember the exact sentence of the first line of that story which said, "The theory that the 'back door' approaches to the fortress island of Singapore are sufficiently protected from northeast attack by natural jungle defences, which are almost as strong as the coastal batteries and protect it from seaward attack, no longer holds good." The story went on to outline a lot of the deficiencies in all our defences, and caused an uproar amongst the Singapore government. They even issued a statement that called my story a *canard*—a word that I had to look up in

Australian troops presenting arms on parade. Harold found them to be in a disgruntled mood, unsure as to why they had been stationed to Malaya. *The Hong Kong Telegraph*

a dictionary to find its meaning. I think the definition is a loathsome type of lie, which I thought was an incredible response as I considered my findings to be important news.

I was continuing to live in the Raffles Hotel, where there were some very interesting visitors from time to time. The first I remember was Sir Charles Vyner-Brooke, who was the white Rajah of Sarawak. He was very worried about the prospect of war threatening his little domain of Borneo, which his family had ruled over for more than a generation. My old friend General Two-Gun Cohen also came to the Raffles Hotel, accompanied by a man called Wong Tai Sin who was the governor of Guangdong Province in China, and had been travelling around on a fund-raising mission for the war in China. I found, however, that life in the Raffles Hotel was proving very expensive, so I decided to move out and find myself a little flat in a building known as the Cathay Building. My room was very comfortable, and there were three other flats on my floor. One of them was occupied by an engineer lieutenant in the Royal Navy whose name was Tom Wall, and like me had served as a boy artificer. The other belonged to an elderly Dutch woman who ran a library in Singapore known as the Blue Circle Library. She was very adept at cooking Malay and Chinese dishes, and in the evenings we used to take turns at inviting each other into our homes and having dinner together.

Work in our office was very busy, and there was always a lot of news coming in and out. In June 1941 we had a report that Hitler had invaded Russia, which was totally unexpected everywhere in the diplomatic world and changed everything in the Far East. It had only been in 1939 that Hitler had made a non-aggression pact with Russia, and I am sure that had been the thing that had put a stop to the Japanese advance in China.

Though now Hitler had changed his tune, and I felt quite sure that the Japanese would soon go on the rampage in Asia. The Japanese had themselves formed what was known as the "Rome-Berlin-Tokyo Axis." This altered the situation in Indo-China, and we did not know how their government would react. One thing that did result from the Axis agreement was that the Japanese were able to have free access to Indo-China, and they were soon occupying places such as Hanoi and Haiphong in the north of Indo-China, increasing their potential threat to Malaya. It was of some comfort to me then to get letters from Marie, letting me know that both she and Pat were safe. In them she told me about their experiences since leaving Hong Kong, which had initially entailed a rough passage down to Manila in the Philippines. After a short stay there they had then gone onto Sydney, Australia, sailing on the *SS Awatea.*

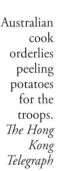
Australian cook orderlies peeling potatoes for the troops. *The Hong Kong Telegraph*

Though in Singapore, every day seemed to take us closer to an attack by the Japanese. I went back for a talk with Admiral Sir Geoffrey Layton, and found that he shared my views about the vulnerability of the island defences. He told me that he had put forward a plan to the British Government that he thought would help us defeat the Japanese, which involved occupying the Kra Peninsula, a piece of land connecting Siam with Malaya. Sir Geoffrey Layton's plan was to travel to Siam and make the government there an offer of oil, which they were short of, but Singapore had in abundance. In return he would ask for permission to garrison the Kra Peninsula with the necessary forces to defend Malaya from a Japanese invasion. The British government had not taken kindly to his idea, which left Sir Geoffrey Layton feeling very angry because like me, he could envisage that an attack could be made by the Japanese from the north. I feel sure, though, that if he had been allowed to pursue it, Singapore would have been a lot more secure, and the ensuing events that happened may have taken a different course.

The Australian government then decided that they wanted to send army schoolmistresses from Australia to India, which was somewhere that Marie did not want to go. She sent me letters telling me how worried she was about the situation, and after much thought I replied by cable that if she did not want to go then the only option left would be for her to resign her position, and she and Pat could then join me in Singapore. That was a pretty hard decision to make given the current circumstances. The situation on the island was becoming less and less safe.

So Marie resigned. I told her that the United Press would pay the air passage for her and Pat to Singapore, and I booked a room in the Raffles Hotel for their arrival so they could experience life in a first class hotel. After their arrival we all stayed there for about a week, and during this time Marie was told that her resignation was not necessary, as there was a post available for her in Singapore as headmistress of a school on a little island off the coast called Blakamati.

She was allotted quarters in the Alexandra Barracks, which were in a very pleasant part of Singapore, and in no time at all we managed to settle in. I also bought an American Dodge car, even though I was unable to drive it, and employed a chauffeur to drive us around. He would take Marie every morning down to the dockside where she would get a ferry to Blakamati Island, and then collect her again at midday to bring her home.

During this time we received a visit from two very well known United Press men. One was Wallace Carroll who had come down from Russia, and was quite a famous name in the newspaper world; the other was a vice president of the United Press whose name was Virgil Pinkley. He was a very nice fellow who we entertained at our house several times, and in return he would take us to a famous restaurant in Singapore called the "Pig and Whistle." But one of the things that Virgil Pinkley most wanted to do was to interview Mr. Alfred Duff-Cooper, a British cabinet minister who had been sent out to be chairman of a war council that had been formed in Singapore. An alliance had been formed between America, Britain and China; we used to call it the "ABCD Alliance," because it included the Dutch as well.

Mr. Duff-Cooper, who was a prominent British politician, arrived in Singapore with his wife, who before they were married was called Diana Manners. She was a very famous stage beauty, and was tall with fair hair.

We arranged an interview at Duff-Cooper's house out near the botanical gardens. Virgil Pinkley and I and Duff-Cooper were sitting down talking, when Lady Diana walked in with a towel wrapped around her head, as she had been washing her hair. She said that she was sorry, and did not realise that her husband had visitors. Duff-Cooper said that it did not matter, that she could stay if she wanted, and so she did. I got the job of helping her dry her hair, while Virgil Pinkley and Duff-Cooper sat and discussed the current circumstances in Singapore.

Australian troops changing the guard at the Battalion Headquarters in Malaya.
The Hong Kong Telegraph

In Singapore the British government was starting to set up what they called a Ministry of Information, which was to be directed by an Australian named Commander John Proud, who had been given a commission in the Royal Navy Volunteer Reserve (RNVR). During the following weeks the Ministry of Information rapidly expanded, and on more than one occasion I managed to get myself into trouble with their censors. However, I was pleased to find within the ministry's staff an old acquaintance of mine called Bob Scott, who had by this time been given the title Sir Robert Scott. This proved to be a very useful contact, because when I did meet with the officialdom of the censors it was Bob Scott who managed to help me out. There was also a man called Ian Morrison, a scholarly chap who had been teaching at a university in China, but the war had driven him out and he had come down and given a job in the Ministry of Information. Ian Morrison was killed years later in the Korean War, and he appears as the central figure in a novel called *Love Is a Many-Splendored Thing*, which was also made into a film.

My poor relations with the Ministry were not helped when Commander John Proud asked me if I would take some publicity photographs for them. He had found out that I had a good camera, and wanted me to use it to take photos of the Malay Defence Corps taking part in exercises, such as crossing rivers and climbing trees. I duly obliged and took three films in total, only then to find out afterwards that one of the sprockets had broken inside my camera and that the films had been ruined, by the same shot being taken over and over again. Needless to say my career as a cameraman came to an abrupt end, and my reputation within the ministry tarnished.

Company of Seaforth Highlanders, formerly stationed in Hong Kong, return from a route march in Malaya. *The Hong Kong Telegraph*

CHAPTER FIVE

Attack on Singapore

The last three or four months of 1941 seemed to fly past, but in spite of the uncertainty over the future, life in Singapore seemed to go on as normal. Marie, Pat and I lived quite happily in our quarters at the Alexandra Barracks, and in the mornings the chauffeur would arrive ready for work. I was, however, aware that events were turning, not only in the Far East but also in Europe. Hitler had already started to invade Russia, and seemed to be progressing through successive invasions of other countries with nothing to stop his will. This news seemed to have a tremendous impact, and under the surface of normality that prevailed in Singapore, a tense uncertainty mounted, with the Japanese now virtual occupants of the northern part of Indo-China and in full command of the ports of Hanoi and Haiphong. I also made a lot of friends inside Singapore, including George Seabridge who was the editor of the *Straits Times*, Singapore's leading daily newspaper, and David Waite, the editor of the *Straits Times* sister paper, *The Singapore Free Press*.

The first indication I received that an attack on Malaya and Singapore was imminent came from a Japanese acquaintance called Johnny Fuji. He was a very amiable and jolly type of character who talked with an Americanised accent, and was also a great baseball fan. One day Johnny asked me if I would like to buy his refrigerator at a knock-down price, which to me seemed a most extraordinary thing to want to do, as there were shortages of food and such an item was extremely useful. I asked him if he was thinking of moving. He was initially evasive in his manner and said that he knew I had been setting up home in the Alexandra Barracks and wanted to give me first option in buying the refrigerator. His story still did not make sense to me, so I pursued with my questioning, and Johnny eventually admitted that he was making plans to leave the colony. He also said that he thought most Japanese residents would also soon be going, and when I asked if he thought that war would soon break out, he said that he was unable to say any more, which pretty much answered my question.

Alexandra Barracks in Singapore, where Marie was allotted quarters after returning from Australia in 1941. *Author collection*

At the beginning of December two large battleships, HMS *Repulse* and the *Prince of Wales,* arrived in Singapore. There was no fuss or official welcome for these great ironclad vessels as they steamed up the Straits of Jahore, and the press were only allowed to report their arrival several days after the event. The *Prince of Wales* flew the flag of Admiral Sir Tom Phillips, who had arrived secretly in Singapore a week previously and taken over the Far Eastern Naval Command from Admiral Sir Geoffrey Layton. These ships, we were told, were merely a vanguard of a newly formed Eastern Fleet, which would eventually consist of a number of heavy ships plus all the necessary auxiliaries. Watching these ships sail in filled me with some exultation, but did nothing to impress Sir Geoffrey Layton, who told me that the ships that had been sent were not the type that were needed. He said that because there was very little protection from the air, two heavy vessels such as this would be left exposed and vulnerable to attack. Instead of this what was needed were smaller more mobile craft that could move in and out from the shore quickly and easily.

On the following day Marie and I had intended to go to the Cathay Theatre to see a film called *Major Barbara*, based on a story by Bernard Shaw. I remember this small point because I had frequently been letting Marie down, after promising that we would go and see it. Opportunities for doing this kept passing us by, because so much of my time was being spent in the United Press office, evening after evening, long after the theatre was closed. It had become a bit of a standing joke between us that when I left in the morning I would say to Marie, "tonight we will go and see it," with the inevitable result, of course, that it would never happen.

On December 2nd we got news of the mysterious and tragic loss of *HMAS Sydney*. By this time the entire Malay peninsula was in a state of emergency, including the state of Jahore where Sultan Ibrahim had made a dramatic overnight proclamation. Volunteer mobilisation throughout Malaya proceeded rapidly and the Regular Army was closed up for instant action, manning coastal stations while the Air Forces under the Far Eastern Command were reported to be "on tiptoes" for any eventuality.

Air Vice Marshall Sir Robert Brooke-Popham, who was now in charge of all forces for Malaya and Singapore, called a press conference for purposes of—"entirely off-record"—allaying what he called "scare reports" emanating from the foreign press regarding the threat to Malaya. For months now I had been investigating the situation regarding the strength of the defences protecting Malaya and Singapore, and been unable to align myself with the unflappable belief persistently voiced by defence chiefs about the unlikelihood of a Japanese invasion. Now with the arrival of HMS *Repulse* and the *Prince of Wales*, along with Sir Robert's unruffled assurances, I began to doubt myself. On this assumption I attempted to summarise the situation once more in a long message to the United Press, which took me most of one evening, only to find afterwards that it had been blocked by a censor. Once more Marie was disappointed, as *Major Barbara* had to be cancelled.

The next thing that happened was a report received from the United

Press Manila Bureau saying that a fleet of 110 Japanese transports, escorted by strong naval forces, had been sighted heading southwards. That report was intended for inclusion in the United Press News Service for distribution in the Singapore press, including our good clients the *Straits Times* and *Singapore Free Press,* as well as several vernacular newspapers. The censors in Singapore blanketed it once more as a "scare report," but I was convinced that it would still be of interest to the naval authorities.

I telephoned Commander Allan Burrows, Royal Navy, who was chief of the Services Public Relations Organisation acting as Press Liaison Officer for the Navy, and told him of Manila's report. "Ha! Ha! . . . that's a good one . . . hundred and ten transports did you say? Must've opened a new box I should say-what! Good old United Press, you certainly like your sensational stuff. Anyway thanks for the dope, Guard . . . but I don't think we need worry very much about it," he scornfully replied to my news.

At the same time, Radio Bangkok was broadcasting an increasing amount of anti-foreign propaganda, and Japan's envoy to Washington, Mr. Kurusu, seemed to be playing for time. Statesmen on both sides of the Pacific were scratching around the bottom of the "diplomatic basket," and Manila's report of the approaching Japanese armada came as the first real rumble of the war machine in Malaya.

However, the situation turned once more, and the gravity of Singapore Island's security was made clearer when Sir Shenton Thomas, Governor of the Straits Settlements and High Commissioner of the Federated Malay States, proclaimed a state of emergency throughout Malaya. The official statement read, "His Excellency, the governor, upon the advice of the military authorities today signed a proclamation calling up the Straits Settlements and Federated Malay States volunteers. This does not signify an immediate deterioration of the situation, but it was decided some days ago that precautionary preparations should be instituted step by step. It means only that the situation is not yet clarified. The Volunteers form an integral part of Malayan defences and their mobilisation can proceed normally without undue dislocation in the community."

The mobilisation included the Straits Settlements Volunteers, the Naval Volunteer Reserves and Volunteer Air Force units, most of which were called up within two hours of the proclamation. Full mobilisation was expected by 4th December, leaving most business houses working with just a bare skeleton of staff. The Police Reserves similarly assumed emergency stations, and tin-hatted policemen and soldiers rapidly appeared at road junctions and protected areas. Meanwhile the regular troops on the northern border of Malaya and at coastal stations had closed up for battle. The Royal Air Force and Royal Australian Air Force received "operational" orders, and were at a state of readiness for any eventuality.

On the same day, General Sir Thomas Blamey, Commander-in-Chief of the Australian Imperial Forces in the Middle East, passed through Singapore from Australia, intending to return to the Middle East after a brief visit to his own country. I met the general in Raffles Hotel. He said he was very confident as to the outcomes of the campaign in Libya where "everything was proceeding according to plan." Regarding the Pacific, General Blamey had little comment to make except to say Australians would like to see a United States naval cooperation in the Pacific. "The salvation of civilisation necessitates all democracies throwing their full weight into the fight. Australians are of the opinion that the United States should throw their Army, Navy and all their resources on our side," General Blamey said, adding "in the long run, a very slow and costly run, they will do so."

The same evening Mr. Alfred Duff-Cooper, British Minister of State for the Far East, who also had just returned from a trip to Australia, received pressmen at his Singapore residence. He said he had been "enormously impressed" by Australia's unified war effort and production. "Even previous conscientious objectors in the New Zealand government view this war differently from the World War which was, they said, 'Imperial,' whereas this war is against the world's greatest evil—Nazism." He had no comment to make on the Far Eastern situation except to remark "I should think so" when asked whether he thought the Japanese government would continue their Washington negotiations. Covering that day's news prevented me again from seeing *Major Barbara* that evening.

Singapore Civil Airport became a protected area and closed to the general public, including the airport restaurant, which was a popular rendezvous for Malayan gourmets. I found out later that there had been more than a thousand applications from domiciled Japanese in Singapore for shipping passages so that they could leave the island. That evening I poked my nose into Japanese affairs in Singapore, and through my own investigations discovered that the majority of big business staffs were planning to leave for Bangkok the following day by steamer while others were booked on the Bangkok Express.

All seemed to be quiet on 5th December, and the main news item was the arrival of the first squadron of Australian-built Beaufort Bombers. Official communiqués publicised the strengthening of the air defences with these additional planes, although they omitted to mention that the new aircraft were only six in number. The mobilisation of the volunteer forces had now been completed, disrupting the operations within many business houses throughout Singapore, and leaving a feeling of unrest throughout the whole of the colony. There was talk of evacuating women and children, and the Asiatic population began wondering whether such precautionary measures would be confined entirely to those of "pure European descent," as was the case in Hong Kong's evacuation in July 1940. I found that the censors suddenly became a lot stricter, and the content of any news stories became considerably thinner.

So we postponed our plans once more, as there was too much of an upset going on and the military seemed to be in a state of panic. The news pot really started to boil, starting early in the morning when the government issued a special decree prohibiting all non-British subjects from leaving Malaya without "special permission." At this time there were already numbers of Japanese businessmen onboard a Thai steamship company's vessel due to set sail for Bangkok at 10:30 am, and they were all ordered back ashore again with their baggage. All naval, military and volunteer weekend leaves were cancelled, and on Saturday morning an official announcement was made saying that further precautionary defensive moves had been taken in Malaya.

In the afternoon Marie, Patricia and I went to the Singapore Swimming Club, which was filled to capacity with the usual Saturday crowd. This had been one of our favourite places to relax, but on that afternoon I just could not settle with the news of everything that had been going on. Overhead there was the whine of the Brewster Buffalo's engines, which by now had become quite familiar, and they seemed to beckon a warning of what was to come. I lay back in a long chair to bask in the glorious sunshine, and closed my eyes and found myself starting to drift into a semi-conscious state. My slumber, though, was very suddenly broken by Pat's precipitous, breathless arrival alongside my chair. She had developed an inherent nose for news and she bore tidings that the *kabun* (attendant in the swimming club) was paging all naval officers and men to return to their ships immediately. I overheard a disgruntled naval officer, who had been dragged from an afternoon siesta, make the remark, "Going to fight the bloody Japs now I suppose."

The Singapore Swimming Club, where Harold first heard that all naval personnel had to return to their ships, indicating that the Japanese invasion of Malaya had begun. *Author collection*

Straight away I got on the phone to Commander Burrows, who was in charge of the press section at the Ministry of Information, and asked him if he could help me compose a cable to tell the United Press office in New York exactly what was happening. Between us we managed to concoct a cable, which left them with no doubt that the Japanese were about to launch an attack on Malaya. On the same day we received back a very swift reply from New York, signed by a man called Fred Fergusson, who I believe was the United Press news editor at the time. It was a very long cable that started off by explaining that the United Press now had a record overhead expenditure, and that they no longer had a "phoney" war in Europe to cover and so wanted to cut down their expenses everywhere. The last sentence that imprinted itself on my mind forever was, "we want nothing, repeat nothing, from your area." It was just as well for them that official sources were now closed up like oysters, and the last word from that area was "Understand General Headquarters expects 'something' within forty eight hours."

I felt very despondent that evening, not only by the reaction I had gotten from the New York office, but also because of the uncertainty that now hung over everything. One good thing that happened, though, was that Marie and I finally managed to get to the Cathay Theatre and found no difficulty in obtaining seats for *Major Barbara*. The cinema was only partially filled, and during the performance a notice flashed on the screen recalling certain sections of the Air Force stationed on Singapore Island. We enjoyed *Major Barbara*, and it was the last cinema show I attended in Malaya.

The next day started with another headache for me, as the antiquated teleprinter that brought the news into our office refused to function at 5:00 am. Our newspaper clients were fuming, as they were waiting for news from the outside world. The Postal Telegraph authorities were unsympathetic, and it wasn't until the afternoon that the teleprinter was put in order and news reports started to trickle in. That unhappy experience caused me to give strict instructions to Arshad, the Malay office boy, that the teleprinter should be switched on and tested at least an hour before the news report was scheduled to start, so that it would give us time to make good any existing defects. Arshad listened to my instructions very carefully, and contritely vowed to follow them out to the letter.

That afternoon an official communiqué almost took all newsmen unawares. "Air reconnaissance over the South China Sea, which has been in progress for several days, has confirmed previous reports of considerable shipping activity and movement of naval vessels including cruisers. The movement is now around Cambodia Point and thence in a northwesterly direction. The reconnaissance was carried out by Catalina flying boats of the Royal Air Force and Hudson bombers of the Royal Australian Air Force. It is interesting to note that contact by aircraft from Malaya was made at a distance of more than three hundred miles." The New York office now suddenly started to take an interest and was querying me regarding the reported landing of Japanese forces in Thailand, which I was able to substantially confirm, but censorship precluded any suggestion of activity in Thailand. "You must understand Thailand is very anxious to maintain neutrality," an official spokesman said while reprimanding me. I thought to myself, "I'd like to know whose side Thailand is going to be neutral on."

In the evening I stuck close to the telephone at home, anticipating that more news would follow shortly. Marie and I talked late into the night, and I was convinced that war would soon be imminent. The last thing I said to Marie before retiring to bed was "when the phone rings next you'll know the war has started in Malaya." At 4:00 am on December 8th the telephone rang. On the other end was a harassed Arshad, who reported, "Oh Sir! The teleprinter is broken Sir!" I angrily said, "How come broken?" Arshad said, "Teleprinter fell off the table Sir!" I said, "What in hell do you mean! How come it fell off the table?" Arshad said, "A bomb Sir! From the Japanese airplane." I was stunned momentarily into silence when just at that moment there was a loud bang near our house and from the veranda I saw searchlights searing the blue-black sky and "flaming onion" tracer bullets streaking towards three silver specks high up.

Whilst I scrambled into some clothes Marie manned the telephone trying to raise transportation for me to the city. Unfortunately my own car was out of commission at that time and as a last effort, having failed to awaken a taxi station, she phoned a colleague of mine who lived nearby, Dickson Brown of the *Straits Times*. Dickson apparently had a bad attack of that "Monday morning feeling," and in spite of the urgency in Marie's appeal for him to rush his car around, Dickson's liver got the better of his news sense and he sleepily told her that he did not "think it was necessary to do anything at that hour," then apparently slipped back into slumber.

So I decided to walk the four miles to the United Press Bureau. The searchlights were still sweeping the sky, but despite this activity there was an eerie quietness all about. Lights were shining in many houses and there

Harold's American Dodge car parked outside the Alexandra Barracks in Singapore, with chauffer and Pat sitting in the back. *Author collection*

were some signs of activity, which was unusual for that time on a Monday morning. I cursed my luck for not having a car available, and was putting my best foot forward when a car driven by a Singapore Air Raid Precautions official overtook me. I shouted after the car, waving my arms wildly, and it pulled up some fifty yards ahead of me. Because of my stiff right knee joint I could not run that fifty yards, but I hurried along with all possible speed whilst the car driver exhorted, "hurry up man! I can't lose a minute."

In the car I ventured a remark to the driver, "Looks as though the balloon has gone up at last." The A.R.P. official replied, "I think it's a practice raid, I knew they were going to have one, but they certainly chose the damnedest of hours for having them!" I said, "But my office tells me there has been a bomb dropped in Battery Road." "Quite likely, we were going to drop some practice bombs, too," said the A.R.P man, in a matter-of-fact way, after which I lapsed into silence until we reached the Singapore General Post Office, as I could see that I was not going to glean any further information. As we approached I could see there was a sizeable crowd gathering on Battery Road, and activity going on with ambulances already picking up casualties. "Pretty realistic practice," I remarked to the A.R.P man as I left his car. The last I saw of him, he was frantically asking a Malayan policeman what had happened.

I made my way to the Union Building, which housed the Services Public Relations Organisation offices, where I found Major Fisher, the military P.R. officer surrounded by a number of correspondents. Fisher was already busy on the "green line," official telephone, and after a few minutes was able to give us the terse official announcement that the Japanese had effected a landing on the Kelantan coast in the northeast extremity of Malaya. I made a quick dash over to the Cable & Wireless office and flashed a message over the United Press circuits, keeping in mind what I had been previously told about cutting down expenses. My message, comprised of just twenty-five words, stated that, "Officially Jap troops landed northeast Malaya." The Pacific War had started.

From the Cable & Wireless office I hurried to the United Press Bureau on Battery Road, which by this time had been cordoned off by police. I had to fight my way through a crowd and argue my way past the police to reach the Bureau where Arshad had reinstated the teleprinter. The morning report was coming in, bearing tidings of the Japanese assault on Pearl Harbour and the Philippines. For the next hour or so the U.P. telephone line was running hot, while I found out as much news as I possibly could from both official and unofficial sources.

Out of the initial welter of conflicting reports the following facts emerged. First, Japanese troops attempted a surprise landing at 1:10 am in the northeast extremity of Malaya near the Thai border. This attempt was repulsed by Imperial land troops after which Japanese planes from aircraft carriers in the south and north flew over various parts of Malaya bombing indiscriminately. Secondly, reinforced Japanese troops again essayed a landing, which this time was successful. The first official report said, "The enemy is infiltrating and converging on Kota Bharu aerodrome." Thirdly, at least three bombs fell in Singapore city, the first falling within thirty yards of the United Press Bureau; some casualties were reported, with the first fatality being Raymond Lee of the Chinese Volunteer Section. Fourthly, Japanese troop transports were massing off the northeast coast of Malaya where they were being bombed by British planes while additional transports and ten Japanese warships were reported off the coast from Bangkok.

By this time Singapore was awaking to the most fateful Monday morning in its history. Battery Road and Raffles Place, in the heart of the city, were crammed with hordes of people of all races watching the police and A.R.P. workers clearing debris from a block of offices and a big department store, which had moved into new premises less than a month previously. Sir Robert Brooke-Popham then issued his "Order of the Day" at 7:10 am, which stated, "The Japanese action today gives the signal for the Empire's navy, army and air force with their allies in the Far East to go into action with a common aim and common ideals. We are ready! We have had plenty of warning and every preparation has been made and tested. Japan thought she could take advantage of Singapore's weakness. However, now that she has decided to put the matter to a stern test, she will find she has made a grievous mistake. We are confident and our defences are strong. Let us all remember that we in the Far East form part of the rest of the campaign for the preservation of truth and justice throughout the world which we must enter with confidence, resolution and devotion to the cause."

An official communiqué was then issued. "All surface Japanese craft are retiring at high speed while a few Japanese troops left on the beach are being heavily machine-gunned in the Kota Bharu area. This morning's landing occurred at Kemassin, and was followed by infiltration towards Kota Bharu. Large concentrations of ships were observed off Kemassin. One Hudson bomber scored a direct hit on the leading ship, which was set ablaze. The second ship was also hit. A landing was effected at Sebak where contact was made by aircraft and land forces on the beach. Fighting on the beaches is still proceeding. Another Hudson bomber scored a direct hit on a barge carrying Japanese troops up the Kelantan River. There have been no bombs dropped on the naval base. Unconfirmed reports state that mustard gas bombs have been used in the northeastern fighting."

Meanwhile all Japanese domiciled in Malaya had been rounded up. I saw fifteen busloads being taken to the concentration camp on Singapore Island, driving through the city past A.R.P. gangs cleaning up damage caused by the first two bombs. Windows within a two-hundred-yard radius were completely shattered by the blast from the heavy calibre bombs. Overhead I observed an open formation of RAF fighting planes speeding out to sea, while there were unconfirmed reports of naval action off the east coast.

Nothing worked properly, and the communications systems became clogged with a terrific deluge of official and press messages; service censorship disrupted and insinuated itself into an otherwise efficiently functioning civil censorship organisation. A fog of officialdom had now descended over Malaya, which the Service Chiefs apparently mistook for a "halo of efficiency." At 11:00 am it was officially announced that Japanese troops had landed at Patani on the Thai side of the Malayan border. Another larger landing was effected at Singora on the Kra Peninsula, making both Malaya and Thailand under attack. Official reports also revealed that one Japanese cruiser, four destroyers, one armed merchant ship and one transport vessel participated in the first attack on northeast Malaya, where they were engaged by British land and air forces. I also found out that there had been sixty fatalities and one hundred and thirty hospital casualties during the morning's air raid on Singapore, but the censor soon jumped on that one before I could report it.

A later official report said three British aircraft were missing from the morning operations in which three large Japanese transports were set ablaze, in spite of the previous communiqué asserting only one transport participated. Late in the afternoon I learned that Japanese bombers were dropping their calling cards on the RAF aerodrome at Sungei Patani in the northeast extremity of Malaya. I tried to confirm this story through the RAF Press Censorship advisor, a former journalist named Gerald Sampson, but found out later that he did not even know where Sungei Patani was!

Soon the news wires were humming again with reports of heavy fighting around Kota Bharu. More and more Japanese forces were pouring into Singora—we heard unofficial reports that Thailand had ceased fire, thus giving the Japanese troops unhampered entry into Malaya over the Thai border. There was a complete blackout in Singapore that night after a quiet afternoon in the city, and the only thing of note taking place was a considerable exodus of the native population to the country in anticipation of Japanese bombs plastering the city. But no bombs came that night, in spite of there being four air raid alerts.

Even though my first message was lodged with the Cable & Wireless office for transmission at 4:50 am Singapore time on December 8th, it did not reach New York until sometime the next day. Joe Alex Morris, the brother of John Morris and foreign editor of the United Press in New York, signed the message that came back. It said, "Up Jack Pronto!" In other words, they wanted me to send more details as quickly as possible. That was not easy for me to do because Kota Bharu, where the Japanese had landed, was three or four hundred miles to the north, and we were getting scarcely any information through from there at all. What news we did have was that there had been simultaneous attacks on Hong Kong and of course, the dreadful news of the Japanese attack on the American fleet at Pearl Harbour. This seemed to plunge the whole of Singapore and Malaya into a tremendous gloom, with a very dangerous threat being presented by our enemy.

On the following day it became apparent to the correspondents in Singapore that things were not going well for the Imperial forces in the north. Censorship suppressed information, which succeeded only in snowballing rumours that a number of RAF and RAAF fighter planes had been destroyed on the ground during Japanese raids on the north Malayan aerodromes. I heard later from more than one source that on the Monday morning when the Japanese planes were plastering a northern aerodrome, an RAF squadron leader had his squadron ready with engines revved up and pilots aboard waiting to give battle to the invader. However, the squadron was not allowed to leave the ground and give fight because war had not yet been declared, and as a result of this insanity every grounded British plane in that particular aerodrome was blitzed and battered by Japanese bombs and machineguns.

Within the first two days of the campaign it became painfully apparent that the Japanese had already achieved air superiority. Kota Bharu was evacuated, Alor Star on the other side of the north peninsula quickly followed suit, and the aerodromes were rendered untenable. Malaya's puny enough air strength was crippled, and without air support our land forces were forced to commence an endless succession of "strategic withdrawals." The official communiqué issued at 1:00 pm December 9th said, "Since yesterday's noon communiqué the situation seems to have developed as follows: the Japanese have engaged considerable numbers of aircraft endeavouring to attain aerial superiority in North Malaya in order to cover landings in South Thailand. Japanese transports were proceeding down the coast of South Thailand escorted by warships and it has been ascertained that all the transports located on December 6th and 7th are now apparently engaged in these landings on the Kra Isthmus and northeast Malaya. So far there is no information regarding further support for these forces and the condition around the Singgora area is such that the advances will be restricted to the few available roads. Fighting at Kota Bharu is still severe although by noon yesterday a large measure of control had been achieved by the Imperial Forces. Further landings took place yesterday afternoon and very heavy fighting ensued. The situation in this area is very confused." A later communiqué the same day included these classic lines: "Information received from the General Officer Commanding the Philippines, also from Australia and the Netherlands' East Indies states that pre-arranged reinforcement and reconnaissance plans have been fully implemented. It is too early yet to attempt to forecast what the Japanese plan consists however it is indicated that following Thailand's collapse the Japanese are preparing to engage considerable forces in order to control North Malaya. This move has always been foreseen as being very likely, and therefore the disposition of our forces has been designed to meet it."

Singapore's back door immediately became front page news, and the official reports failed to shroud the fact that the northern border approaches were not as invulnerable as the defence chiefs apparently wishfully thought. About this time I became afflicted with ear trouble having previously had a heavy cold. Abscesses then formed in both my ears and for more than a week I was almost totally deaf, which was a painful and inconvenient affliction, but had its compensations inasmuch as I was immune to officialdom's quacking platitudes and smug deception.

As time progressed it was apparent that the Japanese onslaught showed no signs of waning. Official reports admitted Imperial reinforcements were being rushed to the north in order to bolster the defences. I turned my attention to naval matters but the official censors refused even to whisper the name of the Eastern Fleet. I knew they had moved out to sea, because two colleagues, O.D. Gallagher of the *London Daily Express* and Cecil Brown of Columbia Broadcasting System had that day gone to sea aboard HMS *Repulse*. I felt mortified at not being given a chance to make the trip, but again my deafness stood me in good stead—had I heard about the opportunity I would undoubtedly have fought to board the ill-fated warship. It was then that we received confirmation of the crushing news that the two great battleships, the *Prince of Wales* and *Repulse*, had been sunk by Japanese torpedo bombers off the west coast of Malaya. Thankfully Gallagher and Brown both survived that tragic loss, which bowed all heads in Singapore.

Chairman of the War Council in Singapore, Mr. Alfred Duff-Cooper, made an announcement on the 9:30 pm radio broadcast on December 10th. In it he said, "Having looked our losses straight in the face with unflinching eyes and bowed heads in revered sorrow, let us raise our heads and raise our hearts. This is not the first time in our long history we have met disaster and surmounted it. There is something in our nature only disaster can produce. These warships were precious but we have others and yet others being built. A month ago we were not safe. We are not safe now, but in these great days safety seems hardly honourable and danger seems glorious. We British living in Malaya are fortunate in having an opportunity to prove our hearts are stout and our patriotism is as pure as that of our brothers and sisters who have kept the flag flying over the capital of the Empire. Battleships are precious but more precious are the hearts of a great people."

Despite such a rousing announcement, in my opinion, that evening was the darkest hour for Britain in the Far East, and I felt the first tremble in the foundations of British prestige in Malaya. The loss of the *Prince of Wales* and *Repulse* was a numbing shock, as they had represented the figurehead of our defence. My aching deafness and the close darkness of the complete blackout accentuated my misery and I lay wide-eyed throughout the night with a prayer in my heart for those fighting to stem the Nippon flood. But I could not stand still, and I had to get myself accredited as a war correspondent with the military headquarters in Singapore. I was told that I had to wear a uniform, although I had no intention of spending a lot on an expensive outfit, and looked around for a cheaper option.

I found a little shop underneath our office on Battery Road, where I was able to buy a military uniform cap, khaki bush jacket, and some shorts. I had been given a badge with a "C" on it to signify that I was a correspondent, and I stuck this on my cap, so my "uniform" was now complete. After doing this, the first big story that I had to cover was the loss of those battleships, which was not easy because we were not given a great amount of detail about it. What we were told was that Admiral Sir Tom Phillips had gone down with the

ACCREDITATION

THE SERVICES PUBLIC RELATIONS OFFICER,
6TH FLOOR, UNION BUILDING, SINGAPORE.

16th October, 1941 No.
H. Guard Esq. United Press, Battrey Road, Singapore.

I have received a signal from the War Office to the effect that you have been officially accredited as a War Correspondent. Attached is copy of Regulations for Press Correspondents accompanying a force in the field. Will you please send your Pass to these Headquarters and they will be endorsed, pending the arrival of your War Correspondents licence from the War Office.

C.R. Fisk Major.
D.A.D.R.R.

Distribution:-
K. Selby Walker Esq.
H. Guard Esq.
C. Y. McDaniel Esq.
R. Maly Esq.

Letter confirming Harold's accreditation as a war correspondent in 1941, which prompted him to go and buy the "least expensive" uniform he could find to meet with regulations.
Author collection

War Department of Malaya "Pass and Identity Book" issued July 1941, revalidated many times with extensions up to March 1942. This was unnecessary as Harold escaped from Singapore in February 1942 to avoid the invading Japanese troops. *Author collection*

Prince of Wales. Fortunately there had been no great loss of life, and most of the survivors were able to make their way to shore because the two ships were close to land when they were sunk. It was, however, a terrible blow, and one that filled the whole island of Singapore with despondency.

Christmas was approaching, and I remember at this time that Sir Robert Brooke-Popham issued his Order of the Day in which he explained about the Japanese landing. He said that the Japanese had landed in some strength in the north of Malaya, and that steps were being taken to meet the threat. There is one sentence of his that has imprinted itself on my mind forever, in which he said that there was nothing to worry about because the Japanese were "easy meat."

On Christmas Day, Marie, Pat and I were sitting down to have our dinner when a van drew up outside the military quarter. Some volunteers started distributing food supplies, which were to be stored as a contingency against us being invaded. In the cupboard space under the stairs in Marie's quarters they put great stacks of tins of bully beef, and all kinds of tinned food. We also at this time got news that Hong Kong had surrendered to the Japanese, just 17 days after the first attack. Our thoughts went to our many friends that we still had in Hong Kong, including George Baxter, the man who took over my job when I left in 1940. We felt very sad, as we had spent many happy years in Hong Kong, and this added to the growing feeling of gloom.

In the meantime I had little or no idea what was happening in the north of Malaya. We got daily communiqués by the army headquarters in Singapore, but these gave us no true idea of what was going on; they included phrases such as "today we successfully disengaged the enemy," which meant very little to me. A Major Fraser had been put in charge of what was called the Press Corp in Singapore, which was comprised of about thirty correspondents, and we were marshalled around just like the military. We used to receive messages from the army headquarters, and the messages would read something like this, "A sortie of correspondents will rendezvous at these headquarters at 0800 hours tomorrow." It then would go on to give details of transport and rations, and it was presented in a military style language, all of which I found rather comical.

By this time I was very much on my own in regards to the United Press. John Morris decided that as soon as the war started that Darrell Berrigan, who he had sent to help me, should be shifted across to Bangkok where there was no coverage of the war at all. I had some very able help from Wee Kim Wee and Arshad, but I needed someone to handle our incoming news service, so that I could go out and do some reporting. To do this I hired a man called Stanley Jones, who had been the editor of the *Singapore Herald*, a newspaper that had been largely financed by the Japanese. Very often his character had been called into question because he was an occasional heavy drinker, but I knew him to be a very able newspaperman.

So it was that Stanley Jones took charge of our incoming service at the United Press in December 1941. A number of quite "high-powered" correspondents by now had arrived in Singapore to report on the war, many of whom were American. It constantly amazed me that they found so much to write about when I could find nothing at all from the military communiqués we were given. The war was still going on up in the north of Malaya, and the daily communiqués, which were also called "The Situation Reports," did not give much inspiration to write a lot of copy. These American correspondents, though, seemed to sit down and write great copious reports, and I could only arrive at the conclusion that I was not a very good war correspondent.

We now started to get fairly regular air raids on Singapore. All the army quarters were fitted with blackout curtains, and we shifted Pat's bed downstairs from the bedroom into a little cupboard where we thought she would be safer. There was an air raid alarm siren quite near Marie's quarter, and though we had some very alarming moments when this thing would sound, we eventually got used to it. Marie continued to go to school on the little island of Blakamati, and life continued where possible in a fairly regular routine.

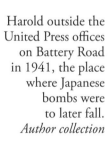

Harold outside the United Press offices on Battery Road in 1941, the place where Japanese bombs were to later fall. *Author collection*

The so-called "Press Corps" was being more and more regimented. There was a young army captain by the name of Henry Steele who was a real "live-wire." He tried to organise parties of us to go up as far as we could into Malaya, but we never seemed to get very far, and going there did not yield much more copy than the daily communiqués distributed to us in Singapore. I began to wonder how I could report on a war that I could not actually see. The war was now nearly a month old, and so far I had not even seen a Japanese, unless it was one about three miles up in the air in an aeroplane!

Christmas had passed, and it was now about the second week of January 1942. News came that the army had decided to evacuate women and children, and so it was that Marie and Pat had to pack a single suitcase each, and board a boat to go back to Australia. Things happened so quickly that I was unable even to say goodbye properly to them, and the last time we were together was in Marie's military quarters in the barracks. I was not allowed aboard ship or even to accompany them down to the quay. It was on that day that I decided I was going to cut loose from the Press Corp, and that I would really go up country and find out what was going on in the war myself.

CHAPTER SIX

Up Country in Malaya

I t was never difficult to get a ride up into Malaya with one of the army units, and the first time I went was on a truck with the Royal Army Ordinance Corp, who were frequently taking up supplies. As we crossed the causeway that connected Singapore Island with the state of Jahore, I could see one of the outstanding sites of the region, the Sultan's Palace. It was a striking view. The palace seemed to be roofed with a translucent green tile that shimmered in the sun, with the Sultan's own personal standard flying above it. He had the reputation of being a rather autocratic ruler, and had a beautiful Austrian or German wife.

I was shocked on my first visit up country by the amount of destruction that was already taking place in the south of Malaya. They were carrying out what was known as the "scorched earth policy," to prevent anything of value falling into Japanese hands. Great stocks of rubber were deliberately being burned, and the tin mines were being wrecked. It must have been a most disheartening sight for the soldiers heading up north to see everything around them being destroyed to prevent it from falling into Japanese hands.

To begin with I made several daily trips, with various units, each time going a little further north, making as many contacts as I could. One day towards the end of January, I was making my way up country aboard an army ordnance unit truck and was greatly surprised to come across hordes of people heading down south. They comprised mainly of Malays, Chinese, and Europeans, and from all different types of background. These people carried with them pitiful amounts of personal belongings; some had hand-carts and others bicycles piled high with all sorts of things. It was a heart-rending sight as there was hopelessness in their faces and they did not know where they were going or what they were going to do. They all had one objective in mind though: to make their way as far south as possible, and away from the advancing Japanese forces.

I remember an elderly Malay man coming to me with a bundle in his hands, saying, "What can I do with these?" He had a little packet of Malay Government War Loan Certificates, in which I suppose he had invested his life savings. So as hopefully as I could I said that with the certificate he could get his money at any time from the post office. "Oh yes" he said, "but the post office has gone!" Another man who owned a beautiful bungalow up country, and who had been in the rubber plantation business for many years, had a hobby of collecting Chinese ceramics. It was a priceless col-lection, but he knew he had to leave, and was going around methodically with a hammer smashing up these ornaments and vases. As he did this he was reciting Rudyard Kipling's poem *If*, and punctuated each line with a blow from the hammer. I also met an English couple who were missionar-ies, and had spent their lives translating the Bible into the various Malay dialects. They were piling all their belongings onto a little handcart, and burning the papers to which they had given a lifetime's work. I felt almost as helpless as these people who were running away from the Japanese.

Sometimes I would spend two or three days up country getting as far north as I could, and then coming back to Singapore to write my stories. One of the greatest shocks of all came one day when I went up country, accompanied by a Reuters correspondent called Bill Henry. We were mak-ing our way to the naval base, and when we got there found it to be deserted. The great King George V floating dock had been deliberately wrecked, and was lying half sunk, with all the machinery in the workshops sabotaged and offices empty. While we were there I even went to Admiral Sir Geoffrey Layton's office, and sat in his chair. The naval base was nothing but an empty shell, and I remember writing my report on his desk, and likening the experience to a visit I had made to Madame Tussauds when I was a little boy, and wondering why everything was so very, very quiet.

I remember on another occasion driving up north with Bob Scott of the Ministry of Information in a big government car, as Lord Wavell, who had overall command of the forces in the Far East, had flown across to Malaya from India to review the situation for himself. I had been told that there was a chance that we might be able to see him at what was called the "advanced headquarters," which was at a place called Selangor. We drove there as quickly as we could, but when we arrived we found that the advanced headquarters had already been evacuated! Some military police there were packing up papers and filing cabinets, and as far as they knew we were already behind the Japanese lines. That is the way the war was moving, and an invisible enemy seemed to be enveloping us. My efforts were being noted though, and I was getting reports by this time from both the New York and London offices of the United Press saying that I was catching all the headlines.

Someone who I did make contact with in Malaya was the Australian General Gordon Bennett, who was the most forthcoming of all the military

Harold, third from right, taking notes with other correspondents from General Gordon Bennett. *Author collection*

commanders that I had met. On every possible occasion I would get to his headquarters, which was always very well advanced up country, to get a personal briefing from him. I remember once waiting outside his hut somewhere near a place called Klang. I was sitting on a mound not far from his hut, when I suddenly became aware that ants were crawling up my legs. While I was sorting myself out some Japanese dive-bombers flew over, and on such occasions they would machine gun everything in sight.

The only thing to do was to make for the nearest slip trench and take cover, but as I had a stiff right leg, I was unable to move that quickly and I didn't think I was going to make it to cover in time. As I hobbled along, though, I suddenly found my feet being lifted off the floor, as a very large military policeman named Bill Rotter picked me up from behind. He ran with me for a distance of about 200 yards, and then flung me into a slip trench and dived on top of me, then shouted in his best Australian drawl, "You silly old cow! Why don't you go home?"

On one occasion Japanese airplanes attacked a little group of us going along a main road, and we all had to scatter. Once more I was not quick enough, and just sat in the middle of the road, making myself into as small a target as possible. While the bullets rattled either side of me on the road's surface, I held my body in and winced. Thankfully the bullets missed me, but as they sprayed into the jungle on either side of the road a splinter was ripped from one of the trees and flew past my leg leaving a deep flesh wound. I had to go to a dressing station, and when you do that in the British Army they take your name and all your details, and I was reported as being a casualty. A day or two afterwards I had a message from New York, which said, "Trust your wound is not too serious." I did not think too much about the wound, but was concerned to find out that the story had been reported by some of the other correspondents, and hoped that Marie would not find about it.

On another occasion I remember meeting up with a group of naval men. They were all survivors of the *Prince of Wales* and *Repulse*, and had formed themselves into a little fighting unit. They had a young commander with them by the name of Reynolds, who wore glasses and had an enormous revolver in the holster of his belt. This commando group was really on the rampage, making excursions behind enemy lines. I would have liked to spend more time with them, but felt it was prudent to make my way south where I thought the final battle would be fought.

During the course of my journey back down through the peninsula I experienced one of the most hair-raising incidents that I can remember during the seventy-one day campaign in Malaya. I had gone as far south as Kuala Lumpur, which is the capital of the Federated Malay States, and decided to stay there for a while to write a cable, as a service was still operating there. One afternoon I went up to the Kuala Lumpur Club, which the local people, I think, used to call "The Dog." It was up on a fairly high hill, and I was surprised that there was nobody else up there, apart from a Chinese boy behind the bar. I asked him for a gin and ginger beer, a popular drink in Malaya at that time. As I was sitting up in this club I looked out on a panoramic view of the surroundings, and could see there were three roads converging on the area. Looking around I could also see rubber piles being burned, and there seemed to be devastation all around. As I looked further into the distance, through smoke from the fires, my eyes fixed upon moving vehicles on the road. I re-focused and then could see that the vehicles were enemy tanks driving down the road!

It suddenly occurred to me that I was on my own, and did not know what to do next. I made my way down from "The Dog" and into the town, and was really taken aback as it was almost totally deserted. In an incredibly short space of time people had uprooted everything and just taken their things and gone. There was a big department store in Kuala Lumpur called Robinson's, and the few people that remained were taking the opportunity to loot the store of anything they could carry. I watched a number of native Tamils coming out of Robinson's with great armfuls of clothing and anything else they could lift. Telephone wires had been cut down and were trailing across the street, and it seemed that Kuala Lumpur was completely cut off and about to be captured by the Japanese.

As I walked further down the street I passed some offices that had written above them the name "Burns Phelps," an importing and exporting company that had an office near our office in Singapore. Instinctively, I ducked into this office, and on a desk found a green telephone, which in desperation I picked up. To my amazement a voice on the other end said, "Burns Phelp. Hello?" I was speaking to their office in Singapore, on a direct line from Kuala Lumpur, in spite of having previously seen that the telephone wires had been cut.

I hardly knew what to say at first, then, just as I started to speak, I saw a tank through the window of the office. There were also British soldiers, some wearing kilts, who started firing up the road with a machine gun. A pitched battle then ensued outside the office, and suddenly I found myself chattering away to the person on the other end of the phone about everything I could see. Meanwhile, outside the window there was bedlam raging for quite a few minutes and then for a moment it all seemed to stop. I waited inside that office until it was almost dark, as I was scared and did not know who or what was outside. Eventually I decided to very carefully step outside, and all around everything seemed to be peaceful.

Suddenly there was a tremendous engine roar, and an armoured car came hurtling around the corner. I found myself being hauled aboard, and to my great relief I found that I was with an Australian film unit attached to the Australian army. A little chap introduced himself to me, named Cliff Bottomly, who was one of the official photographers attached to the Australian Imperial Force (AIF). The film unit were making a run for it away from the oncoming Japanese forces towards Singapore, which was still another two hundred miles away.

More than once we had to run the gauntlet, as there were ammunition dumps on our way being blown up; it was like being in the middle of a gigantic fire works display. Eventually we stopped to rest when it seemed to be safe, and it was obvious that the Australian film crew had also done their share of lifting things out of Robinson's. They had bottles of champagne and many different types of household receptacles that could be used for having a drink. I sat down on somebody's camera case, and drank champagne out of a silver sauceboat. We eventually managed to get back to Singapore safely, and I was very gratified when I learnt from Wee Kim Wee that an office boy from Burns Phelps had brought along my account of the Japanese entry into Kuala Lumpur. It seemed that Malaya was now completely overtaken by the Japanese, although the home of the redoubtable Sultan of Jahore still remained with the standard flying above it.

We were now nearing the end of January 1942, which would prove to be a fateful month for Singapore. Cliff Bottomly was now my constant companion and lived with me in Marie's quarters, which the army had allowed me to occupy even though she had already left Singapore. I remember us sitting on the steps there in the evening of Sunday 9th February, talking about our adventures with the warden for the whole barrack block. Suddenly our conversation was broken by artillery gunfire over in the northwest, and the night air began quivering with gun flashes. Cliff Bottomly decided that we should go and investigate what was happening, so we got into the old Dodge car that I owned and dashed across to the causeway linking Singapore with Malaya.

The scene was one of utter chaos; the Japanese artillery fire was coming from across the Jahore Straits, which at that point was not much more than half a mile wide. The defending soldiers were being literally ground into the mud by the oncoming force, and it was a terrible event to witness. Everyone on that front line was doing their level best, but they were being blasted out of position by the superior Japanese air power and sheer weight in number of enemy troops.

We knew that the tremendous artillery barrage must be the prelude to a Japanese landing in Singapore, and to all intents and purposes we appeared to be in a state of siege. Nobody seemed to know exactly where the Japanese were positioned, and the artillery bombardment could have been coming from some miles into Jahore, though nobody was quite sure. On the following day Cliff Bottomly and I went and took a look from some high land that overlooked the causeway, and as I looked through my binoculars, I was amazed to see the standard was still flying over the Sultan's Palace. I wondered whether the Japanese were there or if they had not yet arrived. We were soon to be disillusioned on this account, as it was on this morning that the British Military decided to blow up part of the causeway, which severed that last link between Singapore and the mainland. We heard later how one of the Scottish regiments, the Cameronians, was the last to march across with their pipes playing "Jeanie with the Light Brown Hair."

At this time I met up with a British Brigadier, who I think was named Bexwith-Smith, and in conversation he told me that this was his "week-anniversary." He had come with the East Anglia Regiment, which consisted of a lot of different units; they had obviously not been equipped properly before they were sent to Singapore, as they were still wearing regulation battledress. Wearing such clothes in a climate like Singapore would be enough to kill a man without the Japanese trying to do so, and I felt really sorry for them. I sat on the running board of the Brigadier's car with him,

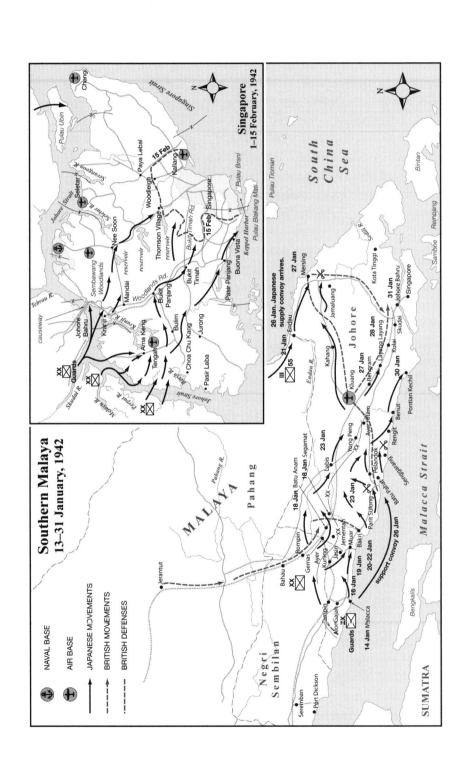

Southern Malaya
13–31 January, 1942

⚓ NAVAL BASE

✈ AIR BASE

→ JAPANESE MOVEMENTS

→ BRITISH MOVEMENTS

--- BRITISH DEFENSES

Singapore
1–15 February, 1942

South China Sea

Malacca Strait

MALAYA

Pahang

Johore

Negri Sembilan

SUMATRA

Singapore Strait

Johore Strait

and told him all that had happened, what I had seen and what had been going on up in Malaya. He was of course very interested, but I was most intrigued when he drew from his knapsack some jam sandwiches and started to eat them. To me this seemed to be most incongruous given the prevailing circumstances, as there were more urgent matters to attend to— a few miles to the north there was an invading Japanese army.

Having taken a look across the Jahore Straits, there was still no sign of the Japanese. Though the bombardments had increased in their intensity, it was obvious that the Japanese were also using their naval units to attack Singapore from the south. The naval bombardments took place in combination with artillery and incessant air attacks, and being in Singapore during those days was a very dangerous and uncomfortable experience. It seemed that the Japanese had been able to make a swift advance down through the Malayan peninsula, and I tried to think about how this had been possible.

The only conclusion I could come to was that there had really been nothing to stop them, even though wherever our armies had been able to contact the enemy they had put up a good fight. The Japanese force was considerably greater than ours, and had more experience fighting in such terrain. Their advance was checked more effectively by the Australians, in the Muar River area, about two thirds of the way down the peninsula. The Australians had ambushed the Japanese, and managed to hold them up for two or three days. I spoke to some of the Australians that had taken part in this, and they told me how the Japanese had eventually come through the rubber plantations on bicycles. So much for the impregnable jungle!

The surrounding areas of the city were now blazing once again as Japanese mortars threw up a solid wall of fire, while planes bombed and machine-gunned at low altitude unhampered. During a period of an hour, three separate waves of bombers blasted our positions at their leisure. I spoke to an artillery sergeant who was directing a twenty-five pounder gun that had been blasting Japanese lines incessantly since Sunday night. The sergeant, grimed black with smoke, cursed the Japanese planes and our lack of air strength. He said, "If we had something to halt their dive bombers we could hold out, but what can we do? How can we work guns when men are being mowed down whenever the Japanese like to do it?" I got second hand reports that Australians from the northern sector were without equipment, and those from the front line told me the troops there were forced to make a quick getaway, abandoning everything. The Chinese volunteers, who were also occupying the northwest sector, only carried shotguns and were armed with nothing but fervent enthusiasm to oppose the Japanese.

I returned to the city and started to write as much as I could about what proved to be my last days in Singapore. It had suddenly dawned on me that most of the other correspondents that had gathered in Singapore were now absent. The United Press in New York then sent me a telegram asking me to write a feature for one of our chief subscribers, the *New York World Telegram*. They wanted me to describe what it was like to spend one day in the besieged city.

I set about this task quite faithfully, and described how in the morning Cliff Bottomly and I got up in Marie's army quarter and made ourselves a cup of tea, followed by the usual routine of going to the Press Centre in Singapore to get the daily communiqué. This as usual told us little or nothing. Then we went down to the ice and cold storage plant on the wharf in Singapore, and managed to get hold of the right end of a leg of pork. We then brought it back to Marie's quarter, so that we could have a roast that evening. During the day I took advantage of a bit of a lull in the siege to do some washing, and boiled my dirty khaki shirts and shorts. While I hung it up on the line, one of the artillery shells came over and landed in a crater nearby and splashed all my washing with dirty mud. I even described how we went to roast the pork in the gas cooker, and that it had blown up, because the gas supply had been cut off and we had tried to light the cooker at the wrong moment.

The story was then handed in to the censors as normal. It was a great shock to me when on the following morning I was sent for by a colonel in charge of the military censors. He said that he was very sorry but I would not be allowed to send any more "signals," which was the army description for cables, and that I was to be investigated by a military tribunal. I then found myself in front of three officers who were questioning me about the story I had written, and they seemed very interested in the piece about the leg of pork! They said, "You describe here the right end of a leg of pork. What do you mean by the right end of a leg of pork?" I said that I always understood a large end of a leg of pork to be the part of a pig from where you got the biggest slices. They said, "How would you describe the other end?" I said that I had not even thought about it. They said, "You weren't thinking about right and left?"

They then went on to explain to me that in their way of thinking, Singapore Island was shaped like a leg of pork, and they accused me of using subtle nuances to convey something in my cables to our offices in New York and London. In other words I was trying to evade the censorship. I was amazed by their findings, but fortunately was saved from what appeared to be a very ugly situation by the intervention of Bob Scott of the Ministry of Information. He explained to them that this was just a harmless feature story, and that I really was not trying to evade censorship at all.

On the following day I got another telegram from Hugh Bailey, who was the president of the United Press at that time. He told me that I should now use my discretion about trying to get away from Singapore, and said that I had achieved the distinction of being the most intrepid war correspondent in this war.

CHAPTER SEVEN

Escape from Singapore

The need for me to escape Singapore was becoming increasingly more urgent, and I was concerned as to how I would find a way of getting off the island. If I needed a reminder as to how urgent the situation had become, I only had to look outside the front of Marie's quarters where soldiers and sand bags had replaced what was once a lovely lawn. After my trip up country I went back to the office on Battery Road to tell Wee Kim Wee that the time had come for me to leave Singapore. He had never let me down the entire time that I was reporting from the front, and quite understood my position. Wee Kim Wee, though, planned to stay on the island with his wife and children in spite of the danger from the Japanese attacks.

I remember on the same day meeting a Mrs. Hosford, who like Marie was a Queens Army school mistress. I was amazed to see her still walking about in the city when clearly the situation was unsafe, especially after all other women and children had been evacuated. She seemed to be quite at a loss as to where to go and what to do, and the only advice that I could give her was to go to the military headquarters to see if they were making any provision for her to get away. To my relief Marie met her some years later at a reunion of Queens Army school mistresses, and found out that she had eventually managed to escape without incident. To me, though, it was quite an incredible situation that she should have been allowed to stay for so long when there was clearly an imminent threat of invasion; it demonstrated the lack of information available for those people that had been left behind in Singapore.

It was now 11th February. Cliff Bottomly and I decided to go to Marie's quarters and get all the tinned food from under the stairs that had been left by the volunteers on Christmas Day. We filled my Dodge motor-car with these tins, and took any clothes we thought would be necessary. I also picked up a carving knife which Marie had bought when she was first posted to Hong Kong in 1926, and which I still have today, in case we got stuck in the Jungle. The next thing we had to do was to find a ship. Captain Henry Steele told me about a "tender" lying idle along the wharf in Singapore harbour that could be requisitioned for our escape (a tender is a small-ish vessel that ferries people ashore from big ships lying offshore). After making further enquiries we managed to put together a "scratch crew," which amongst our numbers comprised an RAF man who was able to navigate. My role was to take responsibility for the engine rooms.

We were now ready to set sail, and we let as many people as possible know that we had a way of getting away from Singapore. I went to see some of the people that I had become acquainted with, including David Waite, editor of the *Singapore Free Press*, but he was quite indignant and said that he did not think it was the time to be leaving. George Seabridge, editor of the *Straits Times* took quite a different view, and both he and his wife were willing to come onboard and take a chance with us. There was also an inspector of police by the name of Pringle, who had a wife and two children. I also looked in vain for Stanley Jones, the man who I had hired to temporarily look after the office.

While all of this was going on, the Japanese unleashed a heavy bombardment on Singapore from both the sea and land. It was a terrible sight. Telephone wires were strewn across the streets and fires blazed from many buildings and the island that we had known so well was now becoming almost unrecognisable. At sea two ships were burning, one of them being *The Empire Star,* which we knew had taken aboard women and children only the day before.

It was late at night in pitch darkness when we loaded most of the people that we had found onto the boat, which included soldiers, RAF men and civilians. I will never forget that at the last moment, Pringle, the inspector of police, suddenly took his family off the boat as they felt it was too dangerous to set sail. They had looked out to sea and been horrified to see *The Empire Star* ablaze, and decided that it would be too risky. There was no time to waste though, and I could not find the time to try and persuade them otherwise. So with no further delay we set to sea with no lights on, and made our way very slowly away from the island.

We had to pass through some very narrow straits at the most eastern tip of Singapore, and it was at this point that a searchlight from the land snapped on, and fixed on us. Within a few seconds there was a loud bang, as a shell exploded about two hundred yards short of us. The searchlight held steady, and then there was the sound of another bang, and this time a shell went over our little boat and fell about two hundred yards to the other side of us. I thought that with a third shell, our attackers would have gotten a fix on us and we would have had it. Miraculously though, the searchlight suddenly snapped off, and we were in darkness again, leaving our little boat to just chug out into the open sea. I remember that it was just at that point when a man on board started to sing "Jerusalem," and there seemed to me something almost miraculous about it all.

Our vessel now found a sudden spurt of speed, and the searchlights remained off, leaving us in an inky darkness. After the excitement of our escape, everyone onboard set about organising themselves with a bed for the night. Cliff Bottomly and I shared a cabin together with a cameraman known as "News Reel Wong." The ceiling of the cabin had large protruding splinters, and in places there were holes that went right through the steel deck above, the result of damage caused to the vessel in the previous week's conflict. One good thing about the holes, though, was that they did provide us with some ventilation, as for most of the time it was sweltering hot and airless inside.

Needless to say, conditions were not conducive to getting sleep. We tried hard to get some rest, in spite of the sweltering heat in our cabin, but I found that any slumber I managed to get was disturbed with images of muddy and bloody brave soldiers defending Singapore. All the time I was also listening out for more shells, and from time to time snapped out of my exhausted naps anticipating another attack, but fortunately they never came.

Nobody seemed to be quite sure in which direction we were heading, but the idea was that we would try and make for Java in the Dutch East Indies. Gradually as daylight broke the passengers had their first chance to look at one another. Someone who I spotted straight away was a military censor with whom I had many disagreements with in the past, and it seemed to me that wherever I went I could not get away from officialdom. There were sixty people onboard our little vessel, which was intended to carry no more than twenty, making everything of course very cramped. Everyone was very tired having spent a night full of fear and trepidation, though there was some amusement created by the antics of a monkey that belonged to a group of RAF men. What food we had was rationed, and our diet mainly consisted of bully beef, slices of bread and sandwich spread. We managed to make a pot of tea, in spite of having no heating arrangements; for hot water we would let steam from the boiler drain into an enamel jug.

Later on in the day our vessel hit the doldrums, slightly halting progress, but we managed to make our way to the Leeway Islands, approximately sixty miles from Singapore. Our captain thought that this would be a good place to hide, as scouting planes had already sighted us in the morning, much to everyone's consternation. At 4:00 pm we got underway again, but it was not long before the ominous shape of three Japanese bombers appeared in the sky. They seemed to know we were there, and circled us three times before eventually flying off. Despite the immediate relief that the bombers had left, some of the RAF men guessed that the bombers were going to load up and soon return, so our captain quickly changed position. His manoeuvre seemed to work, as we did not see the bombers again that day.

It was quite possible that by now the Japanese would have captured Singapore, and our thoughts turned to those people who had been left behind or decided not to leave. There were the Pringles, and also a Mrs. Bailey, who I remembered had the opportunity of leaving but was firmly determined to stay on with her husband, who had been cleaning a rifle and fixing a bayonet to defend his home against the invaders. There were also several soldiers defending homes at the Tanglin Barracks, but to me the possibility of holding out had seemed hopeless. During the night our worst fears were confirmed, when our radioman heard a BBC report stating that three divisions of Japanese troops were on Singapore Island. I imagined Japanese soldiers rummaging through my things, and hoped that they found the three-quarters-full bottle of brandy that I had left on the sideboard, which contained a nasty surprise for them.

Our captain still thought that we were in danger, though, in spite of our location now being somewhere near Sumatra. Once more we dropped anchor near an island, before resuming our journey in a southwest direction. Another sighting of aircraft was made on the horizon, and extra lookouts were posted and gun crews kept on a high level of alertness. In spite of our anxiety, everyone on board managed to keep cheerful, and conversation with fellow passengers was a welcome distraction. I spent most of the afternoon listening to yarns from a Lieutenant Bryan Langley, a war office photographer from Enfield, London and formerly an Elstree Studios cameraman. He was able to give thumbnail sketches of many film stars whom he had photographed, which was a most entertaining diversion. And that is how conversation seemed to be overall, with passengers reminiscing and talking about home life, and I am sure that many new friends were made on our little refugee ship.

The last news we heard from Singapore was that fifteen thousand Japanese troops had landed in Keppel Harbour. It was now Friday 13th February, and our third day at sea. There was very little breeze, and though the vessel was sweltering we still managed to make good progress. At times we were slowed by thick, treacle-like oil slicks that we had to plough through at an agonising crawl. We were fortunate, however, that the sky was full of thick grey clouds, making it harder for Japanese airmen to spot us. During the previous night there was an anxious moment as two convoys passed us and a warship's searchlights swept along the length of our vessel. Though once the danger passed we all settled down and listened to the fine baritone of an RAF officer sing "Land of Hope and Glory."

During the morning our radioman said that the BBC had reported that the Japanese had demanded that Governor Thomas surrender, after they had brought tanks across the remains of the causeway. Some of the RAF personnel said, "Wavell's got his hands full now," thinking that Java would be the next target for the Japanese, with Australia being ultimately where the "last stand" would be fought. I spoke to an Australian captain, who had been in the northwest sector of Singapore during the Japanese landing. He confirmed that his troops had needed to beat a hasty retreat and abandon everything, using their own initiative to find a getaway. The civilian passengers on board now started to realise how lucky they had been to escape at the "eleventh hour."

By 17th February, our brave little vessel reached its destination, Java. The captain carried out a count of all the passengers, which was apparently for the immigration authorities on our arrival. Another Singapore ship passed us during the morning, with women waving greetings, which cheered all our lads. There was much relief on board that we had reached relative safety, and our RAF baritone led the rest of the passengers in singing many of the old favourite songs. A small British naval unit met us, and our vessel waited for permission to enter the harbour.

There was no further news from Singapore, and I was anxious to meet up again with John Morris so that I could catch up with what was happening in the war. It had taken our little boat four days to reach Java, which in normal circumstances would have taken just thirty-six hours. It was not long, though, after our arrival that we heard that Singapore had fallen on the 15th February, so our escape from the island had indeed been a little miracle.

CHAPTER EIGHT

Escape from Java

In Java there was a little United Press office that was managed by a Dutchman called John Boerman, who told me that the Far Eastern manager, John Morris, was one hundred miles further inland at a place called Bandeong. But before I went in search of him, I needed to write the story about my experience of the last days of Singapore, and my eventual escape from the Japanese. After I had completed it I showed it to John Boerman, who warned me that the Dutch censors were very strict, but he told me that he would make sure that my story would be approved. My next objective was to get a proper meal, which would be the first I had had for several days. I booked into a hotel, and after having a good bath went down to the restaurant where I had a Dutch speciality dish of ham steak.

It was now evening and I was more than ready for my bed, having been cramped up in a tiny little boat for days in sweltering hot conditions. I went up to my room and lay down and before long found myself in quite a deep sleep. My slumber, though, was once more disturbed by images in my head of those brave soldiers covered in mud and blood valiantly defending Singapore Island. My ears seemed to ring with the sound of "Roll Out the Barrel," which was the song that the band of sailors who had survived the sinking of *Repulse* and the *Prince of Wales* were singing, as they commandeered trucks to go up into Malaya to meet with the advancing Japanese forces.

The night passed with a mixture of sleep and nightmares, and I was still very tired when the morning finally arrived. I was still in bed when I was suddenly awoken by the telephone ringing in my room, and was amazed when I picked it up to hear Ed Beatty, a United Press correspondent in London on the other end. He wanted to know all about what I had been up to, and so I sat for quite a long time recounting my stories of Malaya and Singapore. It seemed incredible to me that although there had been so much destruction in the Far East, communications were still intact to allow me to take a call directly from London.

Before leaving for Bandeong to meet up with John Morris, I decided to take a look around the area I was in and find out what was going on. I drove to the tip of the island and looked across the straits that divided Java from Sumatra. There was nothing to be seen of the enemy and everything was silent, which made the atmosphere feel a little bit eerie. The beaches around that part of the island looked to me to be ideal for landing Japanese barges, but the Dutch military did not seem to have any real appreciation for the potential threat—it all had overtones of the complacency I experienced in Malaya before it had been invaded.

With that thought in mind I then made my way to Bandeong where the military had a makeshift headquarters, and where the press corps had been gathered. I was very pleased to meet up again with John Morris, and I booked into the Savoy Homann Hotel where he was staying with another correspondent by the name of Bill McDougall. Bill was a nice, hard working young man who had been flown out from New York, and had gained a wonderful reputation covering the war in China. During that time he had even been taken prisoner by the Japanese, but somehow managed to escape and make his way to safety.

We did not have a great deal to work on, as information was once again scarce and not helped by strict Dutch censorship. One morning while staying at the Savoy Homann Hotel I experienced my first Japanese air attack on Java. Everything seemed to be quite calm as we sat downstairs drinking coffee, while waiters were tending to the tables and near us a mother was tending to her brood of five children. Suddenly the tranquillity was shattered as an air raid siren started to wail, and we immediately got up and hurriedly made our way outside. As we did this I noticed that the mother remained seated, while calmly taking her time to drain the last dregs of coffee from her cup.

As soon as we were outside there was droning noise and then a terrible roar as nine Japanese bombers swooped low over the hotel spraying bullets everywhere. Thankfully they did not drop any bombs, but their fire caused us all to run as quickly as possible to the nearest shelter. We got there just as another bomber was swooping down, and we dived through an open window of the shelter in time to avoid the next shower of bullets. As we sat with our backs against the wall breathlessly trying to recapture our composure I noticed to my amazement that the mother and her children who had been sitting in the hotel with us were also in the shelter. How they managed to get there in time I will never know, but they were all fine and the mother was still concentrating on tending to her children, paying little heed to what was going on outside.

Back in the hotel I found out that also staying there was a number of high-ranking military officers, who I think had gotten out of the Philippines when the Japanese attacked. Among them was an Admiral Glassford, who John Morris knew very well, and who was very interested in my stories of Malaya and Singapore. He had the same opinion as me about the defeat and withdrawal of troops from Singapore, in that the Japanese had a superior force in terms of numbers of troops and air command. This view opposed some of those from official sources that thought the Allied defeat was

A Dutch soldier mans an anti-aircraft gun in the Dutch East Indies. *Sydney Daily Telegraph*

both shameful and humiliating. He confirmed that the Japanese had full control of both east and west coasts during the whole seventy-one day campaign, and had been assisted to a large degree by the local population in Malaya, using fifth column methods. Therefore, far from being a shameful defeat in Singapore, the Allied forces that had been left in Singapore had really done a valiant job in holding off the Japanese for so long. I was glad to hear all this from an authoritative figure, because at that time, the world's press were unsympathetic to the surrender of Singapore, which I felt was very unfair.

After a few days John Morris decided to fly out of Java and moved onto Colombo in Ceylon, as we had sufficient staff at the Bandeong headquarters for coverage of the war. This left me in charge of United Press affairs in Java, along with Bill McDougall and John Boerman. The United Press had quite a sizeable bank account in Bandeong, and I told John Boerman to draw all the money from the bank, so that we could divide it between us in case we suddenly needed to leave. I found myself in possession of twenty-five thousand Dutch Gilders, which made me realise that I had not had any money in my pocket since leaving Singapore or even paid any hotel bills since my arrival in Java.

Admiral Glassford invited me and Bill McDougall to his headquarters, which was at a place called Andea, outside Bandeong. His invitation was for us to look through some signals that told the story of the Bali Sea Battle, which had involved four American destroyers that had encountered a very large Japanese fleet, and were eventually sunk. There had been little publicity about the incident, and Admiral Glassford thought that we might be able to make a story from the signals. The papers were very interesting, and Bill McDougall and I became quite engrossed in the story, spending many hours sorting through all the information.

Eventually the time came for us to make our way back to Bandeong, and to our astonishment we found when we got back that the press corps division of the Dutch Army had been completely closed down. Everyone, we were told, had gone down to a place called Tjilatjap on the west coast of Java, where ships had already started to evacuate the correspondents. Bill McDougall and I were the only two correspondents left in Bandeong, so we started to make preparations to make our way down to Tjilatjap to make sure the evacuation didn't leave us behind. I did not know what the

Japanese position was at this moment, and in spite of some sporadic air raids, there had been no reports of any landings anywhere.

It was now 27th February 1942. Tjilatjap was four hundred kilometres from Bandeong, so Bill McDougall and I hired a Peugeot car with a Javanese driver, who we christened "George." We set off from Bandeong at about 2 o'clock, as George said that it would be safer, allowing us to get to Tjilatjap in the cover of darkness at about midnight. Unofficial reports had just started to come through now that there had been Japanese landings on the north coast of Java in the Semarang region. So off we went and though George seemed to know the way, in Java at that time all road signs had been taken down in anticipation of a Japanese landing. We got on very well until dusk began to fall, and George had to stop a few times to ask people the way. It was early evening, after having stopped numerous times, that I started to realise that George was lost. There were no real headlights on the car except for two little blue lights that were compulsory under the blackout regulations, and George had to drive slowly.

When it became quite dark I was astonished to see some lights flickering ahead in the distance, which George thought was the Javanese people coming in from the coast. Despite this we drove on through the darkness, until we came upon a white-washed bungalow with a red tiled roof. There were lights on inside, and so we hid the car amongst some roadside bushes and I got out to go and investigate. As I got closer to the bungalow I could hear a piano playing, and there was a tremendous commotion going on inside. I started to get a bad feeling about the situation, and moved into the shadow to peer around and look carefully through one of the windows.

I have heard people say that when they are genuinely scared that all the hairs on the back of their neck stand up—well that is what happened to me. Inside the bungalow I could see a Japanese officer playing a piano, while another was just picking up plates and smashing them against the wall. For a moment my eyes were transfixed on the scene, and I was petrified. I knew, though, that we had to get as far away from this place as possible, and quickly. So as quietly as I could, I turned and made my way back to the car.

When I got back I reported to the others the dangers that I had seen. George turned the car around and eventually we managed to find our way out to a main road. At this point we had no idea what was going on, but the Japanese had obviously been able to make a landing somewhere, and so we drove as quickly as we could down the main road away from the bungalow using the little blue side lights to guide our way. Eventually we came upon some crowds walking by the roadside going in the opposite direction. Although it was virtually pitch dark, they were walking two abreast, and they reminded me of the people I had seen retreating from the Japanese in Malaya. From time to time they strayed onto the road, and I had to put my head out of the car and shout at them to clear the way, to which they responded by moving back to the side of the road. We saw many of these crowds on our journey, but just ploughed on hoping to eventually reach safety away from the Japanese soldiers we had seen.

By dawn the following day we had arrived at Jogjakarta, where an American squadron of B17 Flying Fortresses were based, having previously flown out of the Philippines. We were taken to see a Colonel U.J. Eubank, who was extremely interested to hear about our drive from Bandeong. He got out a huge map so that we could trace the route we had taken. He pointed out that the Japanese had landed at a place called Serang, which was quite close to the road where we had lost our way. He told us that the people we had seen at the side of the road during the night had probably been captured and were being accompanied by Japanese soldiers. So we concluded that I had been shouting at the enemy from the car telling them to get out of the way!

Bill McDougall and I asked Colonel Eubank if there was any way he could help us escape from Java. The Colonel told us that he originally had seven B17s, but two of these had already flown off to Broome on the northwestern tip of Australia. Apparently the American forces needed to ship out their planes, as they had a similar problem as the air forces in Malaya—they had inadequate fighter protection for their bombers, and at times while they were stationed in Java, some of the Flying Fortresses had needed to take off just to avoid being destroyed on the ground by Japanese air attacks. In spite of this the pilots had not wasted time, had always sought a mission, and in the last days even managed to account for at least two Japanese transport ships from a sizeable fleet.

Colonel Eubank promised to try and get us a ride on one of the five remaining craft, and told us to return to the airfield that night. During the day while we were waiting, Bill McDougall gave me something of a surprise when he told me that he had decided to stay in Java. He told me that he had been sent to Java to do a job, while I had arrived there by accident after escape from Singapore. I tried to persuade him to change his mind, and pointed out to him that a lot of the other correspondents had already left. Bill McDougall, though, was determined and had already made up his mind. The last I saw of him he was driving off in the Peugeot, back to Bandeong with George our driver.

In the evening I got a ride back out to the airfield with some of the air force boys. I waited a long time, but then got the bad news that one of the aircraft that had already flown to Australia had damaged a wheel. A spare wheel needed to be flown there immediately, which meant that there would be no place for me. The next day I spent with Colonel Eubank in a hotel in Jogjakarta, which we spent discussing the war while sharing a big bottle of brandy. As we were doing this we heard news of the Java Sea Battle, in which the Japanese fleet defeated British and American ships. In spite of only having scrappy bits of news it was very depressing, and made me even more eager to get out of Java, as I knew it would now be a matter of days before the Japanese invasion was complete. Another reminder of this fact came immediately afterwards as the Japanese inflicted a terrific air raid over Jogjakarta, and as a result the five remaining B17s were all very badly damaged, which seemed to end any remaining hopes that I had of getting to Australia.

Fortunately though, the American air force got straight into action and started to salvage the remains of what was left of the aircraft. Somehow they managed to cannibalise what was left from the parts of the five damaged planes, and put together two craft which were capable of flying. One was then tested, which seemed successful, and I was told that I would be able to get a flight that night. True to their word, a plane was made available that evening, which was well laden with people. I believe that a normal crew on a B17 is seven people, but on that particular flight there were twenty-nine! Passengers were accommodated by getting down into an area of the aircraft known as the "bomb-bays." We lay head to foot like a tin of sardines, but none of us complained, as we were all desperate to leave Java and knew that the Japanese were not too far away. At six o'clock our airplane started to take off, just as Japanese tanks started to roll into Jogjakarta. There was a rumbling noise outside of the craft, and I believe that

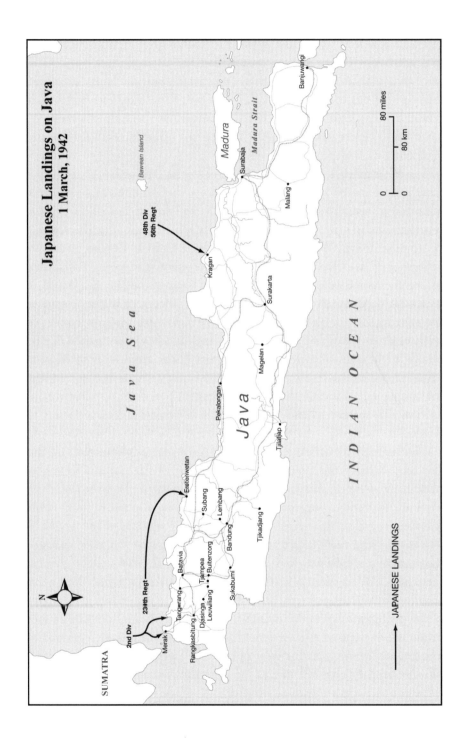

Japanese Landings on Java
1 March, 1942

one of the leading tanks took a shot at us. This was my first ever ride in an airplane, and it was one I shall never forget.

We were still not safe though, as there were plenty of Japanese aircraft around in the skies. Thankfully we were flying mostly in darkness, which, though it helped to hide us, was of little help to our navigator. We managed to fly across the Timor Sea without any further incident, and early the next morning land was sighted, which we knew was Broome in northwest Australia. When we landed on the airfield it was in a state of chaos, as a lot of aircraft had flown out of the Dutch East Indies, including two from the official Dutch airline KLM, as well as the American Flying Fortresses.

After landing, we had to walk quite a distance to a wooden shack where we managed to get some tea, and a bite to eat. It was the first time in quite a while that I had had something to eat, and I was very grateful for it, but what I most wanted was a really good wash. Up in Broome the aeroplanes had stirred up a lot of the red dust that seemed to cover the earth, which the Australians call "bull dust." It is a distinctive red colour, and I was covered in it. We planned not to stay there for too long, but our plane needed to refuel; the only way this could happen was by filling up buckets, as there were no proper filling stations. Eventually we managed to complete our refuelling, and then took off again for Perth.

I was dropped off at the airfield in Perth on 28th February. Looking around for a means of transport, I managed to find a man driving a vegetable truck who was going into town. When we arrived in town I did not know what I would do for accommodation, and asked some Australian soldiers if there was a Red Cross or YMCA in the area where I could get a wash and bed for the night. While I was speaking, a man approached me and asked if there was anything he could do to help. His name was Mr. Silverstone, and was the local manager for Gallagher's Cigarettes and told me that he could help with finding me a room. He took me back to his flat where I was really made to feel at home; I was able to take a hot bath, and his wife then cooked me a steak meal.

In the evening Mr. Silverstone took me to the Perth Club, and introduced me to the secretary who made me feel most welcome and gave me a room for the night. After I had a good night's rest Mr. Silverstone returned to the Perth Club and took me to his bank. I had told him that I had gotten twenty-five thousand Dutch Gilders and wanted to exchange them for Australian currency. I did not expect them to be worth very much, as the Dutch East Indies was in a state of emergency, but to my surprise the manager told me they were worth two hundred and fifty Australian pounds.

I spent eleven pounds of the money straight away on a new typewriter, and then went back to my room in the Perth Club and started to write the story of how I had managed to escape from Java. My clothes were looking rather shabby after all my exploits so I also bought a full Australian military uniform which made me look very much the part of a war correspondent. In all I spent two days in Perth and then managed to get myself booked on a plane going to Melbourne where I had been told that I could meet with the United Press Australian manager, who was called Brydon Taves.

On my arrival in Melbourne I made my way to the Hotel Australia, where Brydon Taves was staying. I found him to be a very serious young man, and he told me that the censors had wanted to see me straight away. I went with him to see a man called Burns, who was the censor based in Melbourne, and I found that he had torn the guts out of my story about escaping from Java. In fact, hardly any detail remained, with no mention of the Java Sea Battle or the B17s. To cap it all my considerably altered story had been sent to the United Press office in New York, from whom I got a reply stating: "Your premature departure from Java left our coverage thinnest." I wondered how premature a departure could be when enemy tanks are firing at you! Though one thing that I found working in my favour was that the other correspondents that had been evacuated from Java from Tjilatjap by ship had only now arrived in Perth. Thanks to Colonel Eubank, and the gallant boys on the B17, I was now well ahead of them so things were not so bad after all.

It was now the beginning of March 1942. I stayed in Melbourne for two days, during which time a lot of people wanted to see me. I had to fight my way out of many invitations to different functions, as I was anxious to get to Sydney, in order to get back with Marie. One appointment I kept, though, was with Sir Keith Murdoch, the big newspaper proprietor who owned a number of different papers, including the *Melbourne Herald*. He was very interested to hear all about my exploits and wanted to get the latest news about what had happened in Singapore. Sir Keith was very interested in everything I had done, and this was not the last occasion that

I would meet with him. I then phoned Marie, and told her that I would be travelling down from Melbourne to Sydney by train to meet her and Pat. I think the train that I caught was called the Southern Cross, and when I arrived in Sydney I found that Marie and Pat were not the only people waiting on the platform to greet me. There was also an enterprising young reporter who had a photographer with him, who took a picture of Marie, Pat and I, and then wrote an article about me describing my escape from Singapore and Java.

Mr. Harold Guard, famous war correspondent for American United Press, greeted today at Central Railway Station by his wife and daughter. Mr. Guard left Java last Sunday after reporting the Hongkong, Malayan and Indies campaigns.

Harold arrives in Sydney at the Central Railway Station, and is met on the platform by Marie and Pat. His arrival prompted great interest from the Australian press, describing Harold as an "Ace War Reporter." *Sydney Sun*

CHAPTER NINE

Australia

I t was absolutely marvellous being reunited with Marie and Pat again, and I looked forward to spending as much time with them as I possibly could. My arrival in Australia seemed to create a lot of interest in the press, as well as with the book publisher Alfred Knopf. They sent me a telegram from their offices in New York asking if I would write a book of one hundred and twenty thousand words "immediately," describing all my experiences in the Far East. At the time I thought this was nonsense as the war was still only three months old, and nobody really knew what direction it had yet to take. Therefore I chose to do nothing about it, and to continue doing my job as best as I could by pursuing any news from where the war was being fought. It did, however, indicate to me how well recognised my reports on the Pacific War had been; for some time it seemed that I was well and truly in the limelight.

An editorial in the *Sydney Telegraph* was written completely about me, in which they called me an acute observer, and accredited me with lots of things, not all of which were exactly true. As I was attracting so much attention, I used this as an opportunity to put a few matters straight on the progress of the war, and also to reply to some criticism that had been made of General Gordon Bennett, who had recently escaped from Singapore. I agreed with the General's opinion that Australia was under a considerable threat from being invaded by the Japanese. However, it was soon apparent to me after my arrival that there was a similar air of complacency about the situation as I had previously found in Singapore and then Java. There seemed to be a hectic whirl of report writing going on within the press regarding anything that the Allied command had to say about the war, but this lacked any real insight, and only seemed to highlight the level of uncertainty there was in these matters. There also seemed to be a lot of "back-biting" and squabbling going on, with the Dutch being critical of the other Allied forces, the Australians arguing with the British who in turn had differences with the Americans. When I was asked for my opinion on the situation I responded that there needed to be a "reality-check" in the country regarding preparations for war.

All around me life seemed to be going on as normal even though the

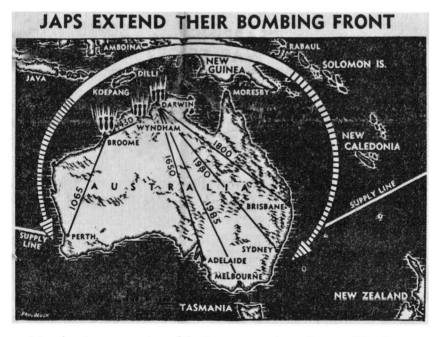

Map showing an overview of the Japanese attacks on Broome, Wyndham and Darwin in northern Australia. The fear in 1942 was that an extension of this 2,000 mile battlefront would cut off supply lines from America and the United Kingdom. *Sydney Sun*

Japanese forces appeared to be only just over the horizon. I was amazed to find a coalminer's strike being threatened, and that the mines might be left idle. With supply lines being threatened, it seemed imperative that everyone in the country pull together to support its industry. How stupid would it have been if Japanese bombers managed to carry out attacks on the mines before the opportunity had been taken to extract as much coal from them as possible? America was offering support to Australia, but it could not be guaranteed when this would actually arrive.

Gradually the realisation began to dawn in Australia that the Japanese threat was getting nearer. Plans were started to ensure that nothing useful was left for the Japanese in the event of Australia being invaded. Demolition was carried out by the military, in the destruction of cars, bicycles and gasoline supplies, and appeals were made to the general public for their cooperation. Australians had already had some experience in such practices during a rapid evacuation that had taken place in Darwin. British employees of the British Phosphate Commission who reached Australia after evacuation from the Nauru Islands told me that preparations there included the demolition of installations that were worth millions of pounds.

In addition to this, over two thousand people had been evacuated from New Guinea. All these events appeared to bring home the seriousness of the situation—the shortcomings of the defences of Malaya and Java were in danger of being repeated all over again. Finally there was an awareness that the Japanese attackers had a large number of skilful fighters who should not be underestimated. Both Australia and New Zealand were prepared to join forces and call up men up to the age of sixty, amounting to an almost total mobilisation of their populations.

I was grateful to be given the opportunity to publicly give my own views on the war by a friend of Marie's, called Mr. Clayton, who asked me if I would give a speech at The Constitution Club in Sydney. In all the big towns and cities of Australia at that time there were branches of The Constitution Club, whose members came largely from the local business community. Mr. Clayton had a son who was in the Australian forces, and I knew that there were many people who were also keen to hear about the conflict as they too had family in the forces. I consented to give a luncheon speech at the club, and when I arrived I was surprised and delighted to find General Gordon Bennett amongst the audience.

I had always found General Bennett to be one of the most honest and forthright commanders in the Far East, and so I was very pleased to be able to stand up in such an arena and defend his reputation. Some people were of the opinion that the general should have stayed in Singapore and fought with his men, but as far as I was concerned he did exactly the right thing in escaping. His expertise in understanding the enemy was of far greater value in helping the Allies develop strategies against the Japanese than remaining in the battlefield and fighting on the front line.

The Japanese were making quick progress now in Java, and were moving rapidly through the islands of the South Pacific. It seemed they were intent on eventually attacking Australia and cutting off the vital supply lines, which forced the Allies to start garrisoning the vast sparsely populated areas of what was called the Northern Territories. Some evacuation of Darwin had already been taking place, with anything that might be of use to potential invaders being destroyed. Many evacuees were also arriving from New Guinea, and Australia now was at a heightened level of preparedness for their potential attackers.

In spite of all these concerns, the remainder of my time in Sydney was very pleasant, and with my newfound fame Marie and I were invited to quite a number of parties. I bought myself some civilian clothes to replace the military uniform I had been wearing since Perth, which made me feel a lot better. After a number of days though, I received a telegram from Brydon Taves in Melbourne asking me to return there immediately. With great reluctance I packed my things and took the train back, as news started to trickle through that the Japanese were now in almost complete control of the Dutch East Indies.

I was also saddened to hear that there had been quite a number of casualties amongst my fellow newspapermen during the Japanese invasion of Java. Among them was Bill McDougall who had tried to get away on a ship that unfortunately sank, and he was eventually picked up by the Japanese. For the second time in his career Bill was a prisoner of war, and I felt terribly sad, as I remembered how I had tried to persuade him to leave Java with me.

We then received news that General MacArthur had escaped from the Philippines, and had arrived in northern Australia on a fast motorboat. We found out that he was going to travel from Darwin down to Alice Springs

Harold's War Correspondent's Credential and Identification Card, issued in May 1942. The nationality on it is noted as being British. *Author collection*

Another War Correspondent's Identification Card, this time issued in June 1942, but this time the nationality has been noted as American. This was a common misconception about Harold, as he was a British correspondent working for an American news agency. *Author collection*

and then make his way to Ballarat near Melbourne. I decided to go to Ballarat and get on the same train that he would be travelling on, and attempt to get an interview with him. My plan succeeded so far as getting on the train, but when I tried to move down towards the general's carriage I found the way guarded by groups of officers. Later in the war I did, however, get to meet with the general, which was an occasion I will never forget.

As I was now stationed in Melbourne, Marie decided that she and Pat would move there from Sydney so that we could all be together again. We managed to find accommodation at Stratton Heights, which was an apartment block overlooking the River Yarra. Once more though, just as we seemed to be settling down I received a message from New York telling me that I had to return to the war front, wherever it happened to be. The war in the Pacific was spreading out over a large area, and it was essential that the Allies try and gain air supremacy over the Japanese. Finding suitable locations for runways was not easy—they had to deal with the heavily forested and swampy terrain of the South Pacific islands or the dry dusty desert of northern Australia. Undeveloped territories also lacked infrastructure, which made supplying any newly formed bases extremely difficult.

The Allies needed to start building airbases, and some land was found at a place called Townsville in Queensland. Even though this was a quiet agricultural area, it had the advantage of having wide areas of flat land for developing runways. From there it was possible for bombers to launch long-range attacks on the Japanese bases, in particular Rabaul in New Britain and Wewak in New Guinea. So myself and a number of other correspondents were booked into The Queens Hotel in Townsville, which was a rather ramshackle affair situated on the waterfront.

Among my fellow colleagues were Byron Darnton of the *New York Times*, also known as "Barney," Bill Kent of the *Chicago Sun,* and Tom Yarborough of the Associated Press. There was no real organisation of the press like I had experienced in Singapore, and scarcely any facilities for us to work in; the press officer in charge of us was also an Australian army dentist. There seemed little for us to report on, and we used to spend most of our time visiting the outlying army camps. Over time a number of other bases were built around Townsville, and though facilities were poor to begin with, they did improve as they became more established.

One evening my fellow correspondents went out to one of the outlying camps at Charters Towers to visit the soldiers, but I had decided not to join them and stayed back at the hotel and continued with some work. I was quietly sitting there reading through some papers when I was suddenly disturbed by our press officer, and dentist, who was excitedly waving a press release in the air. This was the first press release that he had received, and its contents were significant as it contained details of the Coral Sea Battle, which was quite a turning point in the war. The Japanese fleet had been confronted in the Coral Sea by the Allies, who had defeated them, temporarily at least, from advancing towards Australia. It was the first news we had received of this conflict, and I found myself being the only correspondent in possession of this information.

I immediately sat down and started to write a cable to our New York office, but as I was doing so I thought what a shame it was that the other correspondents had missed out on this momentous news. So I wrote cables to their newspapers as well, being very careful to make sure they were all slightly different from each other. For example, in the cable to the Associated Press I described in detail how people had jumped over the side of a stricken Japanese aircraft carrier. I put each correspondents name at the end of the cables and sent them off. On the following day I received a message from New York, asking me if I could match the Associated Press release of people jumping over the side of the Japanese ship, as it was so well written! Of course the other correspondents were very grateful to me, and we all became very firm friends as a result.

CHAPTER TEN

Townsville

Ohne of the greatest friends that I made in Townsville was a 26-year-old lieutenant from the American air force. His name was Christian Herron, and he was a captain of a B26 bomber stationed there, and someone who I found to be a most remarkable young man. Christian, or Chris as he preferred to be called, was slightly above the age of the other pilots, and had at his disposal a motorbike on which he used to give me pillion rides while touring around the local area. This was always a comical sight, as my stiff right leg had to be stuck out at angle from the side as we motored up and down the roads.

The airmen in Townsville were involved with the bombing of Japanese installations in New Guinea, which by now was almost totally under enemy control. Their main target was Rabaul in the Dutch East Indies, and there was a feeling of real determination among the airmen, whose average age was twenty-two, that they were getting revenge for the Japanese attack on Pearl Harbour. These youngsters who were constantly taking to the air were readily becoming veteran bomber pilots, and deadly killers, which was a tremendous pressure for them to live under.

I interviewed one young Private Hugo H. Speir from Minnesota, who at the age of twenty had been attributed with shooting down his squadron's first Japanese Zero. He was only pint-sized and had been serving for seventeen months, and was convalescing from an attack of dengue fever when I met him. Speir described to me an action he had been involved in during April while on a mission over Rabaul. He was an aerial gunner on a medium bomber piloted by a Lieutenant Clarence McClaren, who had been assigned the task of bombing shipping wharves.

When they arrived at their target they immediately encountered heavy anti-aircraft fire, but managed to dive through low-hanging clouds and successfully bomb their objectives. They were heading homewards when Speir observed Japanese fighters taking off. The Zeros caught them up over the sea, and one approached within four hundred yards before Speir blazed away at it with his turret guns. The Zero then sheered off, and Speir was just congratulating himself on a job well done when he saw another Zero swooping up behind the bomber's tail. The bomber banked to the left, but the Zero climbed high and again attempted to approach the tail. The Zero now got within three hundred yards before Speir let fire again with two hundred and fifty rounds. This time he saw the tracers enter the Zeros cockpit, after which the Japanese fighter seemed to be suspended for a while before it wobbled and then spiralled down towards the ground with a trail of belching smoke. Spiers was due to come of age in July, but by all accounts it seemed that he had already surpassed this stage of his life.

Carrying out a bombing mission to Rabaul was by no means an easy task, and a very tiring one. The distances between aerial targets in the South Pacific were vast, which required the bombers to make a stop along the way and refuel. They would fly to Port Moresby in New Guinea, which was over eleven hundred miles away, touch down briefly to refuel, and then take off again quickly to continue their mission to Rabaul. The distance from Port Moresby to their targets was almost as far as the distance they had previously flown from Townsville, and then after completing their missions they had to reverse the whole process again on the return journey. I was very interested to hear about these missions, and told Chris that I would like to take part in one. My interest must have made an impression on him because he went to see his colonel, Hank Sebastian, and asked for approval for me to take part in one of these missions.

Somehow permission was granted, and early one morning I found myself at the airfield being dressed up for a bombing mission. I had a parachute on my back, a gun in a holster around my waist, a full set of instructions on how to use a survival kit, and a big knife for killing any wild animals that I might come across if we should crash in the jungle. All these things were hung on me, and I began to feel like a rather badly wrapped Christmas parcel. After being loaded with all these items, it was time for me to join the rest of the squadron and listen to our commander issue instructions as well as details of the latest weather reports, before strolling out to our waiting bombers.

The propellers on the planes were revving up and spewing biting dust clouds everywhere. I was appointed to Chris Herron's aircraft, and found it a little difficult cramming myself between the radio operator and navigator while laden with all of my equipment. Our squadron comprised eight planes, and we took off late in the afternoon through gathering darkness and into the unknown. Eventually we landed at Port Moresby to refuel, as had been planned, and the whole process was carried out very quietly, quickly, and with as little fuss as possible.

We were up at dawn the next day and our crew once more reassembled, while all around us the noises of the nearby jungle reverberated in the chill tropical air. Once more the propellers were being revved up, and almost simultaneously the first light of morning began to break. With our engines roaring we hurled down the runway and held our breath—it was always a tricky business taking off with a full load of bombs onboard. Our craft, though, gradually lifted off the ground and headed high towards the thick clouds above us.

Chris had a complete air of confidence about him as he took the roaring bomber high over the clouds, and we flew into what seemed to be a new world of yellow gold sunshine with a cotton wool floor. As we settled into a period of steady flying, Bombardier Lieutenant George Barnhill brought me some water in a canteen, along with a 0.45 automatic and phial of iodine, which I was told would not only sterilise a wound but also purify jungle water. I was told to keep these things safely close to me, because airmen had been known to spend weeks in the jungle after being shot down.

I had heard some amazing survival stories of pilots who had needed to bail out. One that I particularly remember involved a lieutenant called Plunkett, who was shot down in his fighter plane by Japanese Zeros that had suddenly appeared from behind the clouds and attacked him. After struggling with his plane, he was eventually forced to bail out at fifteen thousand feet. He did not remember much about the jump, which might have been due to him pulling the ripcord too soon and the shock rendering him unconscious. When he finally came round he found himself sitting in a tree with his parachute entangled in the branches above his head. With a splitting headache Plunkett managed to disentangle the chute and make his way down to the ground.

He then proceeded to hack his way through the jungle using his knife, in a direction that he hoped would take him back to Port Moresby. He took bearings from the sun as he made his way, and checked the saltiness of the rivers for an indication that he was getting nearer the coast. In the end he decided his journey would be made quicker by swimming down the rivers, despite noting along the way the threatening presence of crocodiles in the water and on the banks. He managed to scare off their attention, though, by thrashing at the water, and at nighttime Plunkett would spend his time in the treetops, while around him he could see the glowing eyes of the jungle beasts shinning in the dark.

For days he lived entirely on coconuts, and was lucky enough to encounter some friendly natives who guided him and also provided him with food. One day, though, while swimming the rivers Plunkett suddenly felt a sharp pain in his left shoulder, and when he looked round he saw the nose of a crocodile. He immediately dived hoping to duck under the beast, but the animal did not give up, and clamped its jaws around Plunkett's right shoulder. Remarkably he managed to loosen the crocodile's grip by hitting it with his jungle knife across the nose and then made it to shore. Again he was fortunate that some helpful natives tended to his wounds and got him back on the trail towards Port Moresby.

Peering out at the thick jungle below, I started to think about all the possibilities that lay below for me, and prayed silently to myself that I would not need to use any part of my survival kit. The inside of the bomber was a little reminiscent to me of the inside of a submarine, in that the conditions were cramped, with an array of gauges, meters, noises and the smell of fuel. We were now flying high, at a speed of two hundred miles per hour, and when the clouds broke occasionally we were provided with further glimpses of the thick jungle below and a reminder of our mission.

I examined my parachute nervously, and wondered if I would ever be able to pull the ripcord in the event of us being forced to bail out. For the moment I tried to visualise myself in the jungle with a gun and phial of iodine, but my daydream was broken as our plane dropped six hundred feet.

The plane had plunged deeply as it encountered some air pockets, and the experience was quite nauseating, but Chris managed to steady the aircraft. We then encountered a strong head wind and the skies suddenly darkened, while water started to stream across the windows. We were now over the sea, and we dropped a little more in altitude. The navigator was busy poring over charts and aerial photographs, and the rear gunner took up his position in the turret. The navigator called out that we would be over the target in ten minutes, and Chris asked me if I wanted to sit between him and the co-pilot to get a better view, an offer I accepted. Ahead of us I could see a white cloudbank. Chris decided there wouldn't be time to go over it so instead we travelled straight through it, revealing on the other side Rabaul Harbour laid out in front of us. Looking down on it all reminded me of the type of scene you would find on a picture postcard with the land clearly laid out on the background of a blue sea.

Around the harbour I looked down and could see some large ships along with a number of smaller vessels. We crossed the harbour and then suddenly swooped down low. I looked across at the altitude meter and noticed that it was now registering one thousand feet. At the same time I saw from the ground gun flashes which exploded into black balls of smoke all above and around us. I was startled by a loud cracking noise, which sounded to me like somebody crushing open walnuts. Fortunately there was no obvious sign of damage to our craft, and so we continued to drop in altitude, this time to seven hundred feet. Chris croaked sharply through his throat microphone that our target was now coming into sight. I could now see some long parallel dull coloured buildings, and then our bomb bay doors opened and I was fascinated to see incendiary sticks spread out over a wide area and then explode below us.

Having experienced the exhilaration of the attack, I hoped that we would now make our way back home. The motor roar started to intensify, and we started to climb once more up towards the clouds. Our turret gunner then reported that there was a Japanese Zero on the starboard side, and Chris muttered something under his breath and we increased our speed.

Two more Zeros were then sighted, but we were unable to press the engines any harder as our fuel was running low, and we needed to conserve what we had left in the tanks. In addition to this I also noticed that the temperature needle was now almost touching the redline.

One of the Zeros moved out ahead of us and then climbed high, before turning and swooping back down towards us. I thought that our time had come and that there was no way the Zero could miss us. Chris, however, did not lose his nerve, and with a determined look on his face turned our plane so that we banked down to the right and towards the sea. The Zero was forced to pull out of the steep dive, and in doing so exposed its underside. Our rear guns fired towards the red discs on the Zero's wings, and I saw some of the tracers go to either side while others entered its belly.

We were still plunging towards the water, and I could see military barges below on the surface of the sea. We swooped low again at just seventy-five feet, and I could actually see the Japanese soldiers on the barges jumping over the side as our fire entered the vessels. I looked backwards at the bellowing black smoke and red flame, and it certainly looked as if the vessels had been well and truly hit.

There were, however, three Zeros still paying us some attention as we swooped once more towards the sea. The tail gunner reported once more that two were at our rear, and then suddenly from behind an upper cloud another appeared and hurled itself towards our port side. I heard his guns chatter as he swooped over us, and once more I heard a cracking sound like walnuts being opened. More balls of smoke surrounded us, and our rear gunner swore loudly as his gun began to jam. Thankfully, it freed again just in time, letting forth bursts of fire that sent one of the Zeros zooming away.

At that point there seemed to be a lull in anti-aircraft fire, and only one Zero was now coming our way. Chris narrowed his eyes on the enemy aircraft, and then with a skilful wrist turn we swooped under the oncoming aircraft. Our turret gunner let go with his fire, and then croaked through the interphone, "That's got the bastard!" We then rose once more, and this time we were on our way as the tail gunner started to sing "I Don't Want to Set the World on Fire." The whole business of sighting the target and undergoing the battle took I think about fifteen minutes—it went so quickly that I had barely enough time to be frightened.

The strangest thing then happened. The whole crew suddenly laughed unrestrainedly, and nobody really knew the reason why, but I think it was their way of releasing tension. Chris now began to relax and even permitted me to take the controls for a short while. I felt very proud to be sitting alongside him in the co-pilot's seat as he brought the plane carefully into land. Waiting airmen then hurriedly clustered around our plane as we climbed out with stiff joints to their welcome.

The whole experience had seemed incredible to me, and I timidly asked Chris if it would constitute what he might describe as being a "hot raid." Chris said, "Jeez! I'd say it was! Those tough little babies gave us a run alright, but I think we gave them plenty of trouble too." Everyone seemed satisfied with the mission, though out of the eight bombers in our squadron only five managed to return. We then ate, and drank some newly made iced lime squash, all within the sound of the nearby jungle noises. Afterwards we prepared our beds underneath the plane's bomb bay doors, draping mosquito nets to form a tent. As I put my head down and drifted into an exhausted slumber, I could not help wonder once more what had made the sound of cracking walnuts during our flight.

The next day I arrived back in Townsville, and found that an official communiqué had been issued about the mission that I had been on, which simply stated, "On Thursday morning our Air Force attacked shipping barracks, warehouses and machine-gunned personnel. Incendiaries were dropped on the wharf establishments. The enemy attempted a fighter interception with four Zeros." It went on to describe how eight of our aircraft had taken part in a raid but only five of them had returned, but little other information was provided. I then sat down to write my own story and based it around the communiqué, but also included details about how Chris Herron had dived his aircraft from three thousand to seventy-five feet over Rabaul and attacked the enemy target. I also provided details of how the Japanese fighters had struck at us on the way back, and that we had ended up with more than fifty holes in our aircraft.

I felt very pleased with my finished work, as it really illustrated what it was like on a bombing mission, but as soon as I had handed it in I found myself in the middle of a terrific controversy. Apparently there was a complete ban on any correspondent entering any theatre of war, and this included going on an operational trip in a bomber. Straight away there was an exchange of messages between Townsville and Brisbane and Washington, and it took five days for the censors to decide what to do about me, and also my story.

I was saved by a General George Kenney who at that time was in command of the American Air Force in New Guinea. He said that in his opinion the story was a morale booster to his men, and that if a correspondent was able to go on a mission it should be an encouragement to some of the young men who were involved in these dangerous escapades. After five days I was exonerated from breaking any rules, and my story was at last released, with the headline: "War Ace On Bombing Mission."

So it was that I was able to get involved with these bombing missions, but they were not always as successful as the one I went on with Chris Herron on that first occasion. Raids were going on day and night, and it was sometimes difficult to keep up with what time of day it was. I remember talking to a canteen mess orderly about this, who admitted that he never knew from one moment to another as to whether he had to go and serve up supper or breakfast. However, he also told me that the pattern of the conflict itself would sometimes help him keep track of the days, as he said that on Tuesdays and Thursdays the Japanese would bomb the airfields and on Wednesdays and Fridays they tended to concentrate on the harbour. This he humorously quipped could also help in the planning of the menu, as they could always plan to have fish on Fridays.

Being with the US Air Force meant that days could start at 4:00 am, and never seem to finish. If you were starting in the middle of the night, then it would seem that you had been out all day, but after checking your watch would find that it was only 10:00 am. One particular incident I remember occurred while I was accompanying a night mission, which started with a very bumpy trip in the back of a truck out to the airfield in the company of three Marauder bomber crews. After we finally arrived at the airfield we assembled together in some long wooden huts where coffee and toast were served, which was much appreciated in the early hours. I felt somewhat in the way all of the time—we sat at long wooden benches to eat and drink, and because of my stiff right leg I had to sit on the end. It stuck out into the gangway, and though I was frequently apologetic about the nuisance that it caused, the lads in this group were very friendly to me and addressed me affectionately as "Guardy boy."

The refreshments in the hut seemed to lift the mood of everyone, which for most of our time together had been quite tense. Within the ranks of these brave servicemen were some quite young lads, and despite their best efforts to be jolly it was not hard to notice the tensions etched upon their faces. Then it was time for us to depart, and once more we trooped out into the inky black darkness of the night. I did my very best to keep up with the rest of the lads, and stumbled at times quite helplessly across the rough terrain towards the waiting bombers on the runway. An arm reached out and guided me towards the plane in which I was to travel, which was to be piloted by a Lieutenant C. McIver. I made a mental note to myself to get the names of the rest of the crew, but figured that there would be plenty of time to do this once we were in the air.

My harnesses and kit were all checked, and it was then time for us to climb up the tail end ladder into the plane. Ours was the first in the squadron to take off, and the engines roared once more as we taxied into position at the end of the runway, which had now been illuminated on both sides by torches. There was considerable jolting going on inside the craft as further manoeuvres took place, and the bumping gradually increased as we made our may down the runway. I looked across nervously at our payload, and prayed that nothing would happen to set them off unexpectedly. To everyone's relief the jolting soon stopped, signifying that we were now in the air. I was able to look outside through a small window, and below us I saw that we were passing over a slightly wooded area at the end of the runway.

Conversations now started up between the crew members, and we were all just getting to know one another when we were interrupted, first of all by a bright glow illuminating the darkness outside, which was then followed by the sound of a muffled thunder clap. The first thought to run through my mind was that one of our engines had exploded, and my thoughts immediately leaped back to considering the condition of our unexploded payload. This thought, though, was soon quashed with the news that was relayed through the interphone, telling us that the mission was abandoned as one of the other planes in the squadron had "cracked up." We were not out of danger though, as our pilot McIver now had the task of flying us back down over the ever-increasing flames below us on the ground.

I began to feel the same prickly feeling on the back of my neck that I had experienced when I came across the Japanese troops smashing plates in that bungalow in Java. I braced myself as the plane once again jolted as we came back into contact with terra firma, before finally coming to a halt. We clambered down from our plane as ambulances and crash vehicles sped towards the site of the unfortunate craft, which I found out later had failed to get off the ground before crashing into the woodland. As we entered the operations room there was an air of gloom and all thoughts were for those brave young comrades who had been lost. I found it difficult to find any words to say, and succeeded in only humbly offering round a pack of Lucy Strikes.

Another frightening time on a night bombing mission occurred when I was onboard a flight with a Lieutenant Millard Haskin. Conditions were particularly poor this night, because as well as having the pitch darkness of the night to contend with, there was also a very hard driving rain that restricted any visibility of the ground. We had been flying high over sea for most of our journey when we encountered a terrific storm that lasted for a good hour. For the entire time we were buffeted about, and it seemed that all there was in front of us were thick banks of grey rain clouds, surrounding us from every angle. There was much activity on board, and our radioman was frantically twiddling knobs and looking intently at the various gauges and dials that were available to him. There was also an increased amount of banter through the interphone by the navigator, the majority of which seemed highly technical and unintelligible to me.

After a fashion I concluded for myself that nobody had any idea as to where we were, and I casually questioned our navigator as to our position. "Up in the air," he retorted sharply, which was a conclusion that I would have been able to reach myself. To everyone's relief though, there was at last some respite when the radio operator finally made contact with someone, somewhere, and outside it was possible to see the blurred lights on land below us. We circled the blurry lights, but soon found ourselves back out at sea again. I didn't know whether this was an expected manoeuvre or not, and began to nervously adjust my parachute just in case. My actions were spotted and the crew joked with me, saying it was probably best that I bail out now so at least they could fix their position on somewhere down below. We had been in the air about an hour longer than originally expected, and the fear was, of course, that we would run out of fuel. But suddenly those blurry lights once more came into view, and we descended through the driving rain. Rain had covered the runway, and it seemed that our landing would almost be as wet as landing in the sea. It was a great relief then to experience the familiar jolting as we came into contact with the ground once more and to safety. It had been, once more, very much a "touch-and-go situation," which could have easily ended in disaster for all of us and reminded me again of the skill that the relatively inexperienced aircrews had to use in order to survive.

CHAPTER ELEVEN

Port Moresby

Back in Townsville I was regularly getting letters from Marie, telling me how she and Pat were settling in quite well, although they were of course looking forward to the time when we could all be together again. Events in the war were now moving very rapidly, though up on the Pacific front, following the Coral Sea Battle, I think there must have been quite a sizeable withdrawal of the Japanese from parts of New Guinea. As a result all the correspondents were then moved from Townsville up to Port Moresby in New Guinea.

I shared tents with Australian and American correspondents in the Papuan jungle along with the airmen stationed there, and the conditions were pretty primitive, and very uncomfortable. Mosquitoes and all sorts of other creatures could turn up in the most unexpected places. At night the insects would make quite a noise and provide another reason for not getting a good night's sleep, but so was the prospect of, at any time, there being an enemy attack. The airmen in the camp used to sleep with their aircraft, and drape mosquito nets from them to form tents. They were ready for action at any moment, and ate when they had time, with only lukewarm water to wash down their food. Conditions were no easier for the men when they were in the air, and having to fly for long periods at altitude. A waist gunner from Iowa, Sergeant Frank McCarthy, told me how cold it could get, and how easily arctic temperatures would penetrate his thick sheepskin lined bombing jacket despite having previously been sweltering in the tropical heat of the jungle. None of this seemed to dampen the men's enthusiasm, though, for waging an unceasing war against the Japanese.

In such conditions I was really glad to be in the same camp with my friends Barney Darnton, Bill Kent and Tom Yarborough. One of my most constant companions was a well-built Papuan boy, who for some reason wanted to attach himself to me. I decided to christen him "Gibson," for reasons I can't remember, and he would address me as "Guard Sa." Gibson was completely naked when I first met him, and so I found him a pair of bright blue trousers from somewhere to cover his dignity, causing him to become known as "Gibson of the Blue Trousers." He proved to be very useful to me because he knew his way around the jungle area, and would travel with me in an old jeep to a lot of the air bases around Port Moresby. I think that Gibson may have been schooled within a mission, as he was very strict with me when I used to swear. "Number one topside, he come this side, and be very angry with you Sa!" Gibson would say this whenever I let an expletive slip, as we bumped our way around the rough terrain in our jeep.

It did not surprise me that Gibson had received some education from a mission, because despite the conflict there were still plenty of missions left in New Guinea. I later met up with an Archdeacon called Stephen Gill, from Sussex in England, who had continued to run a mission under the most trying of circumstances. He had been carrying out his work in New Guinea for nearly thirty-four years, and was very determined not to give it up despite the dangers that befell him. The Archdeacon's mission was situated in the Mambare River area, and he told me that on one particular day he was completing a jigsaw with a young native girl in one of the mission's huts when a Japanese airplane flew low overhead firing bullets everywhere. A trail of these passed right between the Archdeacon and the girl, but miraculously did not harm either of them.

Unfortunately such attacks were not restricted to the Japanese, and on another occasion the same thing happened, but this time the perpetrator was an American bomber, who after spraying bullets everywhere succeeded in smashing the Archdeacon's much-prized barometer. He was so incensed by this act that he went and complained to the nearest band of Allied troops he could find, who happened to be Australians. His protests must have gotten through to the necessary command of these forces, as later on that day another American plane passed over dropping a letter of apology. Despite this, a similar incident happened again, but this time with an Australian plane. The Archdeacon had to take evasive action while he was in the middle of hanging out his washing. After this he was advised by the Allied troops that he should move out of the area, which was becoming more and more dangerous, as the Japanese were using ground nearby as a supply dump.

The Archdeacon had himself needed to play hide-and-seek with Japanese troops on various occasions, when they would come wading down the river. Fortunately they did not venture too far before turning round and moving on towards the direction of Gona. He had also helped to recover a hapless American pilot who had bailed out after being shot down by a Japanese Zero. This pilot had broken away from his squadron's formation in pursuit of an enemy aircraft. Unfortunately for him he had failed to notice that another Zero was underneath him, and with no hesitation it shot him down. The pilot bailed out and landed in some treetops before finally reaching the ground. He only had a compass and clasp knife left from his survival pack, which did not give him many options for trying to survive in the jungle. During the daytime he hid himself within the swamps to prevent detection from the patrolling Japanese troops, and only came out at night to hunt for food. His efforts mainly consisted of throwing stones at coconuts in the trees, which was largely in vain as he was too weak to make the missile reach the treetops.

He arrived at the mission hanging onto a log, after travelling downstream by river. At first some of the natives were unsure of him, but they overcame their uncertainty and brought him ashore. The Archdeacon helped nurture the stricken pilot before passing him onto another mission, from where he then made his way back towards his airbase. When I met him, the Archdeacon was continuing to support the war effort by helping the Allies in giving them his knowledge of the local area and native dialects. He was hoping very much, though, that he could return one day to the location of his own mission so that he could continue his work.

It was just as well for the Archdeacon that he did not come into direct contact with the Japanese, because I heard accounts from other missions that had befallen this fate, and these accounts were not very pleasant. One of these came from a German missionary called Brother Alphonse Wiedmann, who was captured by the Japanese in the Wewak area of New Guinea. He told me that not only did the Japanese rob and plunder from the mission but also killed thousands of cattle that were used for the production of milk, butter and cheese. This was a particularly heavy blow to the mission as they had always been a self-supporting community, and needed the livestock to provide them with food. During the ebb and flow of the conflict, the Japanese personnel staying at the mission would be replaced by others, as new troops came in and out on their way to the next frontline of the battle. Some of the Japanese privates were particularly mean, and killed the natives within the mission after first making them dig their own graves.

Not all of the natives in New Guinea were supportive of the Allied troops though, and this was highlighted to me in the experiences of some of the other missions. One of these involved a Father Arthur Manion, who told me that some natives had taken other natives and missionaries captive, and then taken them along to the Japanese to be imprisoned. Manion had

Papuan natives sitting on the bonnet of Harold's jeep. The jeep was given to him by Shanty O'Neil to get around the Port Moresby area of New Guinea.
Author collection

been forced by the Japanese to use a twenty-ton schooner that he owned to run errands for them, and he believed this had led to rumours that the missions were collaborating with the Japanese. At the same time, he thought that the natives who had participated in capturing others may have been mislead by the Japanese, who had told them stories that implied that the Japanese and Papuans where related in some way through their ancestry.

Another occasion when missionaries came into contact with hostile natives was while they were escaping from the Japanese. This came from the account of a Dutch missionary, Father Anthony Cruysberg, who along with other members of the mission took to the mountains after fleeing from the Wewak area. They spent four months trekking up into the mountains, being lead by an Australian lieutenant called Searson. The mountain areas were a tough terrain, and in some places they passed through areas that had never been visited before by white men. It was in these areas that the natives were hostile, and on occasion would attack the other natives who were in Cruysberg's party, and even killed some of them. Fortunately though, no Japanese troops were encountered, and these missionaries doggedly continued their journey. The sisters within the group insisted on wearing their religious garments the whole time, although for most of the journey they walked barefooted. The party led by the Australian lieutenant

Harold with Papuan native boy "Gibson of the Blue Trousers," his companion who helped him navigate his way around the Port Moresby area of New Guinea. *Author collection*

eventually managed to reach Mount Hagen high up in the mountains, where at last they were able to eat and rest within relative safety. From there they eventually made it to Benabena, where they got on a plane that took them to Port Moresby.

It was now May 1942, and the Australian troops were carrying out a tremendous offensive across the Owen Stanley Mountains, which formed a large ridge practically down the whole length of the country. They were intent on driving the Japanese out from the north coast, and this was an immense operation—the soldiers had to make their way right across the mountains, which were covered with a terrific jungle forest. They planned to make their first stronghold at a place called Kokoda, which was on the other side of the range, and in the course of their journey they made what was known as the "Kokoda Trail." The Australian soldiers had to flog their way on foot over the mountains, building what were known as "corduroy tracks"—felled logs buried in the mud to make a footway for the troops to traverse the difficult terrain.

Harold once more befriending Papuan natives in New Guinea. *Author collection*

At this time I was very sad to suddenly receive the news that Chris Herron had been killed. He had just completed his seventh mission over Rabaul, and the news affected me very deeply. I had during my life witnessed death in many places, but there was something about Chris that got you, and it left me with a great feeling of loss. He had more friends in the US Army Air Corps than anyone else I knew, and he seemed to epitomise everything that was fine and grand about the Americans and what they were fighting for. He had flown more than twelve-and-a-half thousand miles in actual combat in less than a month, and not surprisingly, he had died in the act of trying to save the lives of his fellow crewmembers.

Meanwhile in New Guinea the air activity was unceasing, and there were bombers constantly being sent out to attack the Japanese. We were also receiving a fair quota of raids over Port Moresby, and during this time I learned a valuable lesson. If you were able to see an airplane directly overhead then there was no need to worry, but if you saw them two miles ahead then it was time to duck, as a bomb was already on its way down. I made a lot of friends amongst the airmen in Port Moresby, and in particular, another American pilot whose name was Brian O'Neil. He was a captain in command of a squadron in Port Moresby, and was known as "Shanty O'Neil." In civilian life he had been a bit of a playboy. The son of a millionaire family, Shanty O'Neil had attained some notoriety in peacetime when he had flown his own aircraft, and landed it in the middle of a baseball pitch. Shanty O'Neil was a very successful pilot, and went on to be awarded with a Distinguished Service Cross for "extraordinary gallantry in leading a strafing mission" over the Bismarck Sea. I found him to be a very generous character, and was lucky enough to accompany him on a bombing mission in a B26 a year later.

The location of the war front was to change for me once more. I had taken part in twenty-two operational bombing missions, but the United Press had told me that my reports on them had started to lose their news worthiness. From my own point of view the air was very much where the war was currently being waged, and it was far more useful for me to concentrate my time in this area, rather than stumbling my way around in the jungle with my stiff right leg.

In spite of all the previous accolades I had received for my reports from the air, the United Press wanted me to return to Australia, and they were quite insistent with their instruction. I thought that their decision was a great shame, as not only had I been given the opportunity to witness firsthand bombing missions from the cockpit, I was also able to hear many amazing stories from the pilots and crews. One of these involved a Private

Loading report for one of the many bombing missions that Harold accompanied. Example shown is for 22nd Bombing Group, a mission leaving Garbutt, northern Australia on 22 April 1942. Harold is listed as a passenger. *Author collection*

First Class Turrentine from California. He was a nose gunner in a Liberator and had been out on a mission, successfully shooting down between sixteen and twenty-four Zeros. On the return flight though, sixteen more Zeros that had apparently been providing cover for some Japanese bombers, intercepted his plane.

Turrentine told me about all of this, and his story was corroborated by eyewitness accounts from Australian troops who were on the ground at the time, and who eventually helped in recovering the stricken nose gunner from the jungle. The Zeros attacked the Liberator's tail over Benabena as it was unloading a payload of bombs. At this point Turrentine had managed to hit quite a number of them, but then his pilot tried to take evasive action by turning upwards into the clouds. In spite of this, two of the Zeros managed to get above the Liberator and then turn into ninety-degree dives, after which one of the Australian eyewitnesses saw the plane catch fire. Turrentine said that he heard the interphone report that there had been a fire in the bomb-bay area of the plane while he was in the middle of shooting down another Zero that was attacking him head on. He then saw his co-pilot bailing out, but unfortunately his escape was hampered by his parachute getting caught up on the plane's radio antenna.

Turrentine told me that at this point he was scared to death, but he somehow managed to force himself out of the plane's emergency door.

After that, he said he could not remember much of anything that happened, and thinks that he probably lost consciousness, which could have been the result of his plane exploding in the air behind him as he made his exit. Turrentine said that he was in such a hurry that he didn't even have time to pull his ripcord—despite this he found himself coming round in midair with his chute fully open, floating and drifting over the thick forest of the jungle. As he looked around him he saw that there were five sections of his exploded Liberator lying beneath him. As if matters could not get much worse, a Japanese Zero then flew at him, firing shots for some minutes. Turrentine was literally a sitting target, but he managed to evade the attentions of the enemy craft by continually pulling on the shroudlines to adjust his position in the air.

He finally landed in a dried out creek bed, where he was eventually found by natives. They were followed by some of the Australian troops, who found while helping to recover Turrentine from his predicament that his parachute was covered with a film of oil. This could only lead them to one conclusion: that the chute had been blown open by the explosion of Turrentine's own Liberator plane. After further recollection Turrentine thinks that the first action with the Zeros took place at ten thousand feet, and that he must have then bailed out at about six thousand feet. Amazingly, apart from suffering from shock and a few minor injuries, Turrentine otherwise looked to me to be in remarkably good health. I do not know what the chances are of an event like this happening, but I found his story to be quite incredible.

Another story I heard involved a Captain L.J. Kneeskern, who spent seventeen days in the Papuan jungle after bailing out of a photographic reconnaissance plane. He had been photographing the Markam River area when the weather became rapidly worse, and the decision was made to return to base straight away. During the course of poor weather, one of the fuel tanks ran dry, and all of the craft's instruments behaved erratically. The plane started to spin and loose altitude, and so Kneeskern took the decision to bail out. While doing so he believed that he might have pulled his ripcord too soon, as he felt a tremendous wrench on his back, which was sufficiently strong enough to break the jungle knife in his pack. Despite suffering from cuts to the head, which he thinks were inflicted by hitting it against the planes antenna, Kneeskern managed to manipulate his parachute down towards a small stream. His parachute got caught up in some trees, which he estimated were about seventy-five feet high, but despite suffering from a great deal of pain in his back, he managed to shin his way down with his jungle pack in tact. Conditions in the jungle were extremely unpleasant. There was relentless forest rain, which did little to provide him with any comfort; nevertheless, he managed to sleep for a short while with the help of some morphine from his pack.

Kneeskern had to stay in the same position for three days as his pain became worse, after which time he managed to crawl to the nearby stream to quench his thirst. He then decided to use the stream as his vehicle for making his way through the thick jungle, despite seeing numerous crocodiles in the vicinity. Through wear and tear his pack and uniform gradually started to disintegrate, and he needed to make repairs to them on several occasions over the next five days. Opportunities for him to eat anything of substance became limited as the matches from his survival kit had become sodden in the river, and prevented him from lighting a fire over which he could cook a meal. Just when he thought there was no hope in sight, he saw two natives at the foot of a mountainside. Kneeskern managed to get their attention by calling out to them, and then slide his way down towards their direction. Thankfully they were friendly, and could also understand enough pigeon English to understand him and to bring him some food. They then took it upon themselves to canoe him downstream towards a plantation station, where Kneeskern's wound could be dressed by some Australian troops. From there the natives then took him further down river, where Kneeskern was finally met by someone who took him back to base. His escape from his stricken aircraft was quite remarkable, as was his survival in the jungle with the support of the Papuan natives.

It is, of course, very dangerous to be at altitude without an oxygen mask, but I heard a story about a Private Wilbur Browne who somehow managed to defy this requirement. On a bombing mission, he took off his mask at altitude on more than one occasion to go and assist his injured comrades. During the mission both of the side gunners on his craft were injured, and so he removed his mask and left his own position as radio operator to go back and give them assistance. He also adjusted their oxygen masks and tended to their wounds before calmly returning to his original position. Browne then noticed that the tail gunner had collapsed right at the end of the craft, and guessed that this may have been due to a frozen oxygen mask. Once more he removed his own mask, and made his way back through the craft to assist his stricken crewmember. At great personal risk to himself he tested the tail gunner's mask and provided artificial respiration, leaving himself vulnerable for more than two hours. Browne certainly defied all the odds in his actions, and exhibited extreme bravery.

Another story I heard concerned a Spitfire pilot named Philip Goldsmith, who was defending Darwin. He told me that he had been attacking a Japanese bomber, and had managed to destroy its cockpit before finding that a Zero was pursuing him. Though he was able to get the Spitfire's speed up to four hundred miles per hour, while performing various twists and turns, he could not shake off the enemy craft. The Zero started to fire at him and completely shattered his cockpit hood, with all the pieces from it imploding onto his lap. To make matters even worse, while being blasted by the wind in his unprotected pilot position, his joystick then came off in his hand. Goldsmith's memory of events faded at this point but he believes that he then exited the cockpit. He was aware that he was hanging out of it, but was then blinded as blood was forced into his head. The next thing that he recollected was being in seawater with his parachute fully open, forming a canopy over his head. He managed to fight his way clear of it, and then inflate his rubber dingy. Goldsmith believes that he was about forty miles off the coast, and remained stranded there for twenty-four hours, during which time he only had two fruit tablets to survive on and was visited by a six-foot sea snake. Eventually he was picked up by an Allied rescue craft after being spotted out at sea by aircraft. This was just another example of an amazing escape from a distressed airplane, where there seemed to be little hope of survival for the pilot.

I also heard about some rather unusual crewmembers who belonged to a US Marauder bomber group. One of these had the name "Cocky," and was a white Australian talking cockatoo. He belonged to Private First Class Hank Colvin of Missouri. Hank had also previously owned a kitten called "Blackie," who had frequently accompanied high altitude heavy bombers and was provided with oxygen during what had amounted to fifty hours of combat time. Unfortunately Blackie went the same way as many other airmen, when he did not return from a mission that Hank was not on. Blackie's demise left a big gap in Hank's life, and so he bought Cocky.

Apparently Cocky was quite a nervous crewmember during his first missions, and sat nervously on Hank's shoulder incessantly glancing right and left. Hank would soothe Cocky's nerves by saying to him, "what's the matter boy," and after subsequent trips the bird started to settle down to life in a Marauder bomber. In fact Cocky became quite blasé about the whole experience, and would squawk angrily at the ack-ack gunfire that burst near the bomber and continually scream, "what's the matter boy." Cocky had unfettered freedom around the camp, and on one occasion sat on a squadron commander's shoulder when he was delivering an address to his crewmen and repeated his line "what's the matter boy."

Back in Australia the Americans had formed what was known as the "Brisbane Line." This was a line of military defences stretching from Brisbane on the east coast of Australia, right across the whole of the continent down to Perth in the lowermost western corner. The immediate objective of this had been to protect the southeastern corner of the country, where the major cities were situated. The Americans were also busy developing the road systems in the Northern Territories of Australia in order to improve communications and supplies to these remote areas, and the United Press wanted me to go up into these remote areas to find out how the development of the defences were progressing.

I had to make contact with the Australian army in order to make this journey possible. Luckily at this time they had just put into service a new radio communications vehicle that was like a large caravan, full of radio equipment, which was making a trip from Adelaide in the south all the way to Darwin in the north. One of the tasks of this vehicle's crew was to test out radio frequencies and transmit conditions in various parts of Australia, and I was able to join them in their journey.

As I was attached to the American forces I had to let them know about my forthcoming project with the Australian army. One of the standing orders in the American army for anyone going into the northern territories of Australia was that they had to take with them special equipment. As a result I was suddenly laden down with a bunch of special equipment, including a mosquito net, Parang, various types of boots, and lots of other paraphernalia. In fact there were forty-two items altogether! I had to travel to Melbourne with this great load and then down to Adelaide where I was to join up with the radio communications unit.

CHAPTER TWELVE

The Northern Territories

I arrived in Adelaide by train and much to my surprise, as we pulled into the station, I could hear my name being called out over a loud hailer, asking for me to report to the stationmaster's office. With great intrigue I went along to the office, and was surprised to find a fully uniformed chauffeur standing there waiting for me. I found out that he had been sent by a Mr. Lloyd Dumas, which was a name that I had not heard before, but who turned out to be the proprietor of the leading newspaper in Adelaide. Apparently Sir Keith Murdoch had telephoned him and requested that he take good care of me.

The chauffeur had been given the instructions to take me to the Adelaide Club, which was one of the most exclusive clubs in Australia. So we loaded my American army kit into the back of the car, and off we set. When we arrived at the club I was greeted by the head porter with all the aplomb of a celebrity. The Adelaide Club was a bit like living back in Victorian days, as I had a very old-fashioned, beautifully furnished bedroom, and at breakfast the meal was always served in lovely silver dishes. There was a long story written about me in Lloyd Dumas's newspaper, and this proved to be something of an embarrassment, because as a result I was invited out by the Press Club of Adelaide and given the most wonderful lunch where everyone had too much to drink, including me! I walked back to the Adelaide Club after that lunch in a very "fuzzy" state of mind. We had been drinking what the Australians call "plonk," which I don't think is a very high grade of wine. At the club the head porter said there had been a telephone message for me, asking me to call a number. To my surprise I found that I was speaking to Government House, and after a while I was put through to a Lady Muriel Barclay-Harvey, who was the wife of the Governor of South Australia. She asked me if I was able to go to lunch on the following day, and because of my state of mind I said yes. Then there was an awkward pause, and I found myself saying, greatly to my horror, "What are you going to have?" She said, "Oh! What would you like?" So I said, "Roast beef and Yorkshire pudding," and she laughed quite loudly over the phone, then said, "Well! You will have it!" On the next day in a rather shamed faced way I presented myself at Government House at the appointed time, where I had the most delightful meeting with Lady Muriel Barclay-Harvey and the Governor of South Australia. Also at the lunch were a bishop and an Australian naval captain, and it was a most enjoyable occasion. We had a good laugh about me ordering my lunch of roast beef, which was on the menu, and it was delicious.

I was glad though, to eventually escape from Adelaide, as the hospitality became too overwhelming. When I reported at the Australian military depot in Adelaide to pick up my communications unit, I managed to persuade them to look after the equipment that had been placed upon me by the American army. They rolled it up into a huge bedroll, put my name on it and said they would send it on to me. We then drove from Adelaide in South Australia, up to Alice Springs, which is just about in the centre of the country. It was there that the Great North Road, or "Burma Road" as some called it, started and then stretched for nearly nine hundred miles all the way up to Darwin. This road was being constructed to provide a supply line to Darwin to help protect it from Japanese attacks, and it required hundreds of tons of soil and gravel so that it would resist the torrential downpours experienced during the rainy season. There was a set time limit of ninety days for the completion of the road, and it was actually finished in eighty-seven. It cut through what was marked originally on the maps as complete desert. It was a great asset for a newspaperman to be travelling in one of these communications vans, because I was able to sit down and write a story that could then be radioed to Australian military headquarters in Brisbane or Adelaide. This was a situation of mutual benefit to the Australian army, because through me sending my stories, I was helping them test out their equipment.

Our communications van was part of a convoy of vehicles making the trip up to the north. When we reached Alice Springs I stayed in the Stuart Arms Hotel, which is the same hotel that General MacArthur stayed in when he escaped to Australia from the Philippines. I had a long talk with a chambermaid, whose name was Sarah Long, and asked her about the impression she got of him. She said, "One thing you get here is clean beds, good food and that's all the MacArthur's asked for. Like all Americans they liked steak and eggs for breakfast—roast beef and steak is about all the Americans eat. Missus MacArthur was a lovely little woman and the little boy was a darling. I used to collect all the small Australian coins for Arthur, he had a big collection of tiny coins and liked three penny bits. I thought he was a horrible man. The way he used to talk to his wife and son!" We did not stay long in Alice Springs, and travelled further north, from which point the desert really began.

I remember one of the first things we came across was the Devil's Marbles, which are perfect spherical stones about ten feet in diameter, piled in pyramids, and nobody knew how they had gotten there. Even more curious was the small velvety green-leaved plants that grew from the granite rocks, which the natives called rock moss and which resembled edelweiss from the Swiss Alps. Around us stood the occasional Goanna observing our movements. These impressive looking mini-dragons had originally been imported to help rid Australia of the incredible swarms of flies that invade this part of country. From this point we travelled for miles along a straight road that stretched off into the horizon, where the sky seemed to meet with a miraged ocean. The journey was quite monotonous. The drivers would constantly recount stories in order to keep their wits about them, as it would be too easy to fall asleep and run the truck off the road and get bogged down in the desert sand. At various points along the way we stopped at staging camps, where vehicles were refuelled and checked over and also gave us the chance to rest and eat.

Our party was being lead by an Australian Sergeant called Allen, and he knew quite a number of survival techniques for living in the desert. He had lived in the outback for the best part of his life, and he showed me how to make a meal in the middle of the desert. This first of all involved setting light to a Spinifex bush, and then placing on top of it a slab of Mulga wood. Onto this you then could cook a piece of meat or even a pancake. Meals were always accompanied by "Billy Tea" brewed in a "Billy Can," which is actually just an ordinary can with a wire handle. You put this on the fire until it boils, then take the Billy Can off the fire and put the tea in. The Billy Can is then left so that the smoke from the fire blows across the can, and then it is swung around, and only the force of gravity holds the contents in. The brewing of Billy tea is quite a fine art.

On one occasion we shot a bush turkey, and after plucking the bird we boiled it for almost eight hours in a kerosene barrel, then roasted it over a fire. It cut cleanly, and was just as tasty as the turkey you might have at home for your Christmas dinner. I also learnt how to wash and shave from just the water in an enamelled mug. To do this there has to be two of you. First you can damp your shaving brush and lather your face. Then you shave flipping the lather off into the sand, after which you rinse your face very sparingly with the remaining water. Then you get your "cobber" to slowly trickle the rest of the water over your neck while your head is held forward. It is amazing how much washing you can do with just one mug of water.

The first stopping place on the Great North Road was Tennant's Creek, which was a little one-horse town. There was a wooden shack there that was meant to be a branch of the Bank of New South Wales. It was from Tennant's Creek that our communications van then set off into Simpson's Desert. Ninety miles into this desert we came across a man living in a cor-rugated iron shack, who I sat down and talked to. He said his name was "Buzzer," and that he'd been sitting there for months, sifting the sand for little grains of gold that he was collecting in a little bag. Every now and then he would take his bag into Tennant's Creek, where the Bank of New South Wales would give him vouchers in return. He would then set off back into the desert to sift for more gold. In the desert we came across some amazing sites: ant hills that were twenty to thirty feet high, looking like some Middle-Eastern town with mosques and minarets. The bull dust would be whipped up into whirlwinds that the Australians called the "Willy-willys."

As the convoy made progress we passed through various outback town-ships, but the further north we travelled the more the civilian population began to dwindle. I left the convoy for a period of time at one staging post, to hitchhike off the "beaten-track," and found American troops carrying out the construction of defences in these remote areas. I travelled hundreds of miles, passing through cattle stations and mining areas on the way.

I eventually reached an American army outfit, where the soldiers were performing all kinds of miracles in the arid desert, boring for water, from which it was possible to cultivate various crops. In one place they even managed to grow watermelons! Some of the troops had also made contact with the native Aborigines. One in particular was an American lieutenant called Tom McCord, who was among the original American forces that were destined for the Philippines, but were then diverted to Australia after the Japanese invasion engulfed the islands in that area. The camp in which he was stationed consisted of drab pyramid-shaped tents that were typically found in many military concentrations. In amongst these were numerous gum trees, and it was here that the "Burma Road" finally finished.

Tom McCord was on very goods terms with the natives, and they looked upon him as someone that they could come to with all sorts of problems. He was in charge of this camp, which had an advanced railhead that was performing the vital role of supplying Australia's northern de-fences. The supplies were transported by an 1860 vintage locomotive that the Americans called "Spirit of Protest," in a parody of South Australia's "Spirit of Progress." Though nobody underestimated the importance of the role of this locomotive in supplying advanced bases where it was im-possible to do so by road.

The work that was going on did not just involve the building of the infrastructure, but also in helping the airbases maintain their craft. I met a Lieutenant Paul Hellwig from California and Lieutenant Maurice Richards from Colorado, who ran what was described as "Bush Aircraft Manufacturing Incorporated." This was an Air Corps service squadron whose meritorious work had become a byword throughout the Northern Territories' airbases. They directed operations to maintain combat aircraft in action, which had initially involved servicing a small squadron of P40 fighters, but had increased in scale as the war progressed. The increase in Allied air strength meant that they now had to maintain and repair giant

Liberator bombers, with little change being made to their available personnel and maintenance equipment. One of their number, a Major M.H. Miller who had serviced Ford and Douglas airplanes since 1928, told me, "this is the best outfit I've worked with anywhere. They do everything and some repair alterations and additions are actually factory jobs carried out right here in the bush. Planes get shot-up and damaged and are seemingly beyond repair, but this squadron doesn't let anything halt them. They know what's needed and if they haven't got it they just go ahead and make it."

Bush Aircraft Incorporated also included a complete parachute department, who found time to also repair soldiers' uniforms. These repairs were effected using an antiquated Singer sewing machine that had been salvaged from the wreckage of bombed out buildings in Darwin. Further resourcefulness was taking place with instrument repair, where seemingly unusable airplane instruments were being converted into testing equipment to check airplane parts that would otherwise require factory repair. Repair Testing Manager Harry Baylies told me, "some bombers don't have very good luck, but we always manage to make good use of every salvageable scrap metal, and anything we don't have we just make it. Everybody is improvising here while awaiting the arrival of necessary equipment and improvisations often prove the best."

McCord did everything that he could to help the natives—one of his medical staff had even carried out a caesarean operation on a distressed Aboriginal woman. The Aborigine men would regularly confide in him about their problems, and often made their way across to the camp to seek his advice. McCord took me to meet the Aborigine tribe one evening, which was a most entertaining experience, as they put on what is called a *corroboree* and daubed themselves in white clay paint. They did some fantastic dances for us, and then laid out a feast of soup made from Kangaroo tail and meat that had been cooked in the hot embers of the desert sand.

While I was in the outback the troops also held a rodeo, which was somewhat nostalgic for many of the Texans amongst their number. Many of the Americans took part in the event, some who were revealed as first timers by being thrown to the ground by their steers. Some, though, were near professional riders, and had been keen to get to the event. They rode for miles through typical Australian cattle country in a variety of vehicles, ranging from jeeps to six-wheel trucks and old style buckboards. Despite the Americans expertise though, the Australians proved to be victorious in the event with their superior knowledge of the steers. Even the Americans admitted that the Australian steers were hard to control, particularly during the buckjumping contests.

I managed one day to witness an Aboriginal kangaroo hunt, which demonstrated the native's ingenuity and capability to live off the land. A wrinkled ancient member of the tribe dubbed "Smiler," and his youthful spear-carrier named "Tommy," walked swiftly out into some bushland, while I pursued them in a beaten up old Chevrolet. They walked for almost five miles, when Smiler suddenly stopped, and signalled to Tommy to do exactly the same, while he raised his head and peered into the far distance. He stealthily moved forward, seemingly sniffing the air, and when I looked further into the distance a large buck kangaroo could be seen.

I halted the car and watched Smiler approach the kangaroo, which once or twice raised its head to look enquiringly around. Each time it did this Smiler stopped and stood still, before proceeding again, until he was just twenty yards from his quarry. He then raised his skinny arm and launched his unwieldy spear. The kangaroo toppled, and Smiler and Tommy danced round in circles, and ran over to claim their prize. The unfortunate beast was then trussed and slung onto the spear between Smiler and Tommy before it was carried back to the reserve for undoubtedly a triumphant feast. Later on I declined the offer to eat the "sizzled" heart and liver, and left Smiler to devour these "titbits" with the rest of his tribe.

The American's achievements in the Northern Territories were quite amazing, and they managed to build a strategic road system through Australia's interior, allowing many more motor truck fleets to travel throughout previously unexplored parts of the country. After travelling through northern Australia's seemingly illimitable outback, I was left with the distinct impression that the potential of this land was vastly underestimated. My thoughts were confirmed by a camp sergeant at an Australian staging post. He was formerly a resident of South Australia, and told me that for ten years prior to the war the geography text books in the school where he taught made the northern part of the country appear to be something like the Sahara Desert. However there were many areas in the north where there were green pastures and an abundance of water for those who knew where to find it. At another staging camp, where the geography books had illustrated the land as being a wilderness, six Australian soldiers managed to cultivate three acres of vegetables.

There were many fascinating aspects to Australia's Northern Territories, but what the United Press really wanted was a story about how the war was being fought from these areas. I managed to locate in my travels some heavy bombing and fighter groups, which unexpectedly presented me once more with the opportunity for taking part in a mission. This arose when I learned that there were raids being planned on Sourabaya in Java, which was an interesting trip as it entailed the longest journey so far in the war, to the Southwest Pacific. From the air base in northern Australia to the target was twenty-one hundred miles, and the bombers to be used in these missions were B24s, which were bigger than the Flying Fortress.

I was extremely keen to get involved in the missions, but initially I was told there would be no room for any additional passengers as fuel had to be preserved on such a long flight. Then, however, a possibility suddenly presented itself. On a B24 they used to carry a very large photographic camera, called a K2 Camera, which fitted into a circular aperture in the floor of the bomber. This was used to take surveillance pictures, and when it was finished with, the camera could then be removed and replaced with a machine gun. I managed to get myself on some training flights to learn how to operate the K2 Camera, and was very pleased when I was eventually told that I was proficient enough to take part in one of their missions.

The mission on which I was involved made a journey to Sourabaya, and was most interesting, as we flew over the South Sea Islands. Our navigator was able to explain what was below us during the flight, in the same way that a travel courier would with a crowd of tourists. He would point down to some islands and say, "that's where the Kokoda Dragons are" (there is a legend that some giant lizards as big as dragons lived on one of the islands). We also passed over the Timor Sea that looked a beautiful blue colour, and was very tranquil.

Finally we reached our target in Sourabaya, which was quite a strong Japanese base at that time, and the excitement within the bomber increased. I got my K2 camera together and hurriedly shot everything in sight, until I reached the end of the eighteen-exposure film. Some Japanese Zeros then suddenly appeared and attacked us, so I removed the camera as quickly as I could and started to replace it with the machine gun. As I was doing this the aircraft suddenly took a sharp turn. My balance was not that steady with a stiff leg, and the sudden movement was enough to make me stumble back and fall onto my backside. At the time I was still holding onto the camera and its weight helped to push me down until it finally hit me in the face. The oxygen mask I was wearing protected me from the blow, and in the midst of the fighter's attack I scrambled as quickly as I could to my feet and put the machine gun into place. But by the time I had gotten myself sorted, there was nothing left to fire at, which made me feel a little foolish.

Our mission had been quite successful however, and we made our return trip without any further incident. After we landed back in Australia though, and I took off my oxygen mask, I found all of my crew members staring at me with horrified expressions. From first impressions it looked as if the whole of the lower half of my face had been removed, as it was completely covered in blood. After cleaning up my face, and on further inspection, the only damage was a small cut on my chin, probably the result of the camera hitting me in the face. Inside the mask though, the blood had nowhere to go, and had just spread itself all over me.

I had to go along with the rest of the crew to the briefing room and describe everything that I had seen. My film was then taken along to the

Harold poses as an aerial gunner in the B24 bomber, on which he participated in the long distance mission to Sourabaya, Java as a cameraman. He operated a K2 camera that interchanged with the machine gun when under fire from Japanese fighters.
Author collection

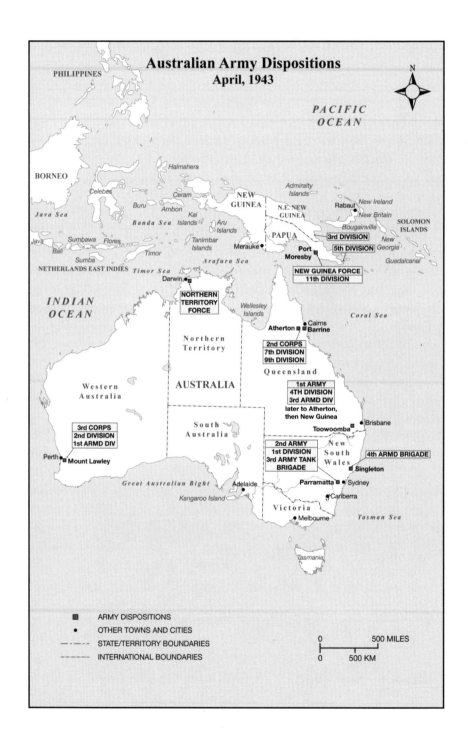

Australian Army Dispositions
April, 1943

N

PHILIPPINES

PACIFIC OCEAN

BORNEO

Halmahera

Celebes

Ceram

NEW GUINEA

Admiralty Islands

Buru

Ambon

Java Sea

Kai

Java

Sumbawa Flores

Ambon

Banda Sea

Islands

Aru Islands

Tanimbar Islands

PAPUA

N.E. NEW GUINEA

Rabaul

New Ireland

New Britain

Bougainville

New Georgia

SOLOMON ISLANDS

3rd DIVISION

5th DIVISION

Bali

Sumba

Timor

Merauke

Port Moresby

NETHERLANDS EAST INDIES

Timor Sea

Arafura Sea

Guadalcanal

NEW GUINEA FORCE
11th DIVISION

Darwin

INDIAN OCEAN

NORTHERN TERRITORY FORCE

Wellesley Islands

Coral Sea

Northern Territory

Atherton

Cairns
Barrine

2nd CORPS
7th DIVISION
9th DIVISION

Queensland

Western Australia

AUSTRALIA

1st ARMY
4TH DIVISION
3rd ARMD DIV
later to Atherton,
then New Guinea

Brisbane

3rd CORPS
2nd DIVISION
1st ARMD DIV

South Australia

Toowoomba

Perth

Mount Lawley

2nd ARMY
1st DIVISION
3rd ARMY TANK
BRIGADE

New South Wales

4th ARMD BRIGADE

Singleton

Great Australian Bight

Adelaide

Parramatta

Sydney

Kangaroo Island

Canberra

Victoria

Melbourne

Tasman Sea

Tasmania

■ ARMY DISPOSITIONS
• OTHER TOWNS AND CITIES
— - — - — STATE/TERRITORY BOUNDARIES
— - - — - - INTERNATIONAL BOUNDARIES

0   500 MILES

0   500 KM

operations room to be developed, but it turned out to be a complete waste of time in every respect. The pictures showed the attacking Japanese Zero fighters miles off as tiny little specs in the distance, and only the corner of some of the land installations that we were supposed to be bombing, and very little else. I felt a complete failure, and somewhat foolish, given my fumbled attempts at replacing the camera with the machine gun.

There was, however, one frame that was of great interest to the American Air Force intelligence people. It showed what looked like a spider in the middle of the picture, which on closer inspection turned out to be a perfect picture of a phosphorous bomb exploding. The Japanese had a trick of sending up a fighter that would race ahead of a bomber, and then drop one of these bombs in front of a bomber. I had managed to get a picture of this taking place, so there was at least something that I could be proud of.

The role of the aerial photographer was extremely important, as they provided about eighty-five percent of the Allied intelligence reports. I met a number of these air reconnaissance photographers, including one called Lieutenant Frank Fosket, who was from Colorado and known by his comrades as "Fearless Fosket." His title was earned with good reason as these photographers had to be fearless; they flew for many miles that could only be covered by a Liberator bomber, in which they would have to stand in exposed positions with no means of personal defence.

He told me that on one mission he was on that the Japanese attack was so fierce that he had to help out by feeding ammunition to the right waist gunner. As he was doing this, the tail gunner reported that his turret had been hit, and then to make matters worse, gasoline started blowing in all over the craft. Number two engine had failed, and number one stalled while the craft was at a thousand feet. Miraculously, though, they managed to regain altitude and the tail gunner started blasting away, and Fosket saw two Zeros go down in flames. But the rudder controls were then found to be damaged, and the plane started to spiral as number one engine again started to stall. The craft load had to be lightened, and ammunition and other equipment were hurriedly jettisoned but this was to no avail, as they continued to spiral down. Finally the order came from the pilot, named Olsen, for everyone to be on standby to bail out. Somehow though, Olsen managed to steer the craft home, which was something of a miracle as the ground crew said they had never seen such a badly damaged bomber make it back. Apparently there were more than three hundred explosive shell holes counted all over the fuselage, with some larger holes indicating it had been hit by heavier calibre cannon fire.

This experience had not deterred Fosket though, and he told me that it was a hell of a feeling sitting in the bomber over a target, with the ack-ack guns firing at you and Zeros flying around. He said that the feeling of vulnerability he got was often wiped away when he came back with some good pictures. Often pictures of target areas were taken from heights of anything between three thousand and twenty-five thousand feet, and Fosket had soon managed to rack up a fair number of combat flying hours. He estimated that he could fly for an average of forty hours per month, and that did not include practice flights.

Another photographer that I met was Taylor Simmons, from Washington, who had been accredited with the finest set of aerial photographs on record during the longest reconnaissance flight over Sourabaya. Simmons, who was formerly an architect, specialised in photo interpretation. In his pictures it was possible to identify almost everything, including the ships scuttled by the Dutch and Americans during the Japanese invasion. Simmons's clear-cut pictures showed the Sourabaya base area in detail, and I was easily able to identify the Oranje Hotel, where I stayed briefly prior to the enemy attack. It was also possible to see the familiar lines of one United States destroyer, which the Japanese had apparently salvaged.

Other snap-shooters of the air include Staff Sergeant George Ashworth, who could claim the distinction of being the only photographer in this area to have sunk a ship while flying over Manokwari. After Ashworth had taken pictures, the bomber made another run over the target, and Ashworth assisted in unloading incendiaries on a small amount of enemy shipping. He scored a direct hit on one craft, which caught fire and sank within a few minutes. Ashworth even found the time to take a photograph of his prize.

Corporal Vincent J. Ewadinger was also a photographer on a long-range reconnaissance trip over Manokwari, and during heavy anti-aircraft fire, smoke from the Liberator's bombs clouded the vertical camera. Despite this he continued to take pictures by lifting the camera (which weighed seventy-eight pounds fully loaded) and taking pictures through a gun port with the help of the waist gunner. The results proved to be perfect, portraying the Liberator's direct bomb hits on the pinpointed target area with huge smoke columns rising up. The pictures were considered to be so dramatic that the commanding general personally ordered five sets, and I believe one picture was also used for a cover of *Life* magazine.

It was now August 1942, and I had my 44th birthday with this bombing group up in the Northern Territories of Australia. The boys had gotten some barrels of beer, but keeping them cool in the incredible heat proved to be almost impossible. They managed, however, to find a way round this, by taking a couple of the barrels up in an airplane to thirty thousand feet for more than two hours—this was very effective in cooling the beer off, but I dread to think how much this cost in fuel and American taxpayer's money! My assignment in the Northern Territories came to an abrupt end though, with a message from Brisbane. I was told that I had to return to New Guinea as soon as possible, where things were now apparently moving on very quickly.

CHAPTER THIRTEEN

Wau (Wow)

So I packed my things once more and flew back to Port Moresby late in September 1942, and soon found myself back within an old familiar crowd. To my amazement one of the first people to visit me was Gibson of the Blue Trousers. Somehow the news of my arrival had reached the bush telegraph, and there was Gibson to say "Guard Sa!" Once more we took off in a jeep to visit the surrounding area to see how things were developing.

One Sunday afternoon, Gibson and I were out in our jeep when we came across an American transport group who were taking American soldiers up to a place called Wau (pronounced wow). Wau was one of the key targets in New Guinea where the Japanese were quite heavily installed; it offered the benefit of being on high ground clear of the jungle, and was a very important strategic area. One of the things that intrigued me about Wau was its name, and I envisaged all sorts of headlines with the word Wau in it. So I managed to get myself on a flight heading up to Wau, which was an exciting prospect as there was no flat land for planes to land—the runway there was literally on a hillside.

The airfields in Wau had successfully been protected by Australian troops, but on the flight that I took, American troops were being sent there to provide additional support. Our pilot for the trip was Captain Pears Jacques, who I had met before when he was shuttling American Air Corps out of Java to Broome. The circumstances this time were different. Instead of retreating from the Japanese, the Allied forces were starting to hold and push the enemy backwards, which was something that made Jacques very happy. Our heavily laden plane took off into the glaring midday sun, and rapidly gained altitude above the cotton wool cloudbanks that rapidly built up over the Owen Stanley Mountains during the afternoon. The plane, christened *Barbara Ann,* was part of a squadron, and onboard the other aircraft I could see the faces of soldiers peering apprehensively down at the thick jungle country that was virtually impossible to travel through by foot.

Flying through the Owen Stanley Mountains' gorges in formation is a tricky business, and I had a bird's eye view of the countryside while standing between Jacques and his co-pilot. The thickening cloudbanks and treacherous twisting gorges precluded any formation flying, as the proximity of other planes in the squadron became increasingly hard to judge. Jacques took us down a few hundred feet, which brought the forest-clad mountains well within view on either side, with tiny native villages in seemingly uninhabitable regions clearly visible.

We were now starting to reach enemy territory, and the whole crew kept their eyes and ears open. I asked if there was any fighter cover for us, to which I was told by a sergeant peering at our cloudy exterior surroundings, "Yeah, I guess they're up there somewhere." We continued to zoom between the sandstone walls of the gorge, and in places derelict mining machinery could be seen. Jacques told me that we were getting close and that the Japanese were now beneath us, which was something he knew for a fact having previously been fired at during his morning run.

We emerged from the gorge, and Wau appeared suddenly in front of us like a picture postcard. Jacques pointed out the runway, which seemed to be tilted at a forty-five degree angle, and remarked that the runway could sometimes be a little "ticklish" during takeoff. We circled and watched other planes in our squadron landing, before we ourselves swooped round to land amongst the eager Australian soldiers.

Our stay at Wau did not last too long, as there was some fighting going on in the area. A lanky green-clad Australian captain took the time to lend me his binoculars, and pointed out a twisting brown road approximately a thousand yards off in the distance. Through the glasses I could see a column of slowly trudging uniformed Japanese infantry, whom the Australians had done battle with that morning. Another Australian officer commented that from the way the Japanese were moving he was expecting another fight to take place during the night. He said that it was amazing how the enemy troops just kept coming, and that they appeared to be dug into the mountain like a colony of ants.

When the time came to leave we said our farewells to the Australian troops, exchanging cigarettes, news of the war and good wishes. Then off we soared back into the sky, after bumping along the angled runway. Wau's importance was made even more apparent from the air, with it's aerodrome strategically placed, and it was hardly any wonder that those brave soldiers were fighting so hard to defend it. Jacques took the plane over the twisting brown track and pointed out to me the column of Japanese marchers. He swooped low over them, and I would have approximated there were about two hundred troops amongst their numbers along with two grey covered vehicles. As the enemy soldiers gazed up at us, we regretted not having a good-sized bomb to drop on them. Further along the mountain we passed Japanese garrison huts, with wispy smoke from the kitchens wafting in the air and figures scurrying around under the shadow of the airplane.

Soon though, we were back among the considerably thickening cotton wool cloudbanks. These were testing conditions for Jacques, who had already flown ten hours that day, although he was happy to do it, as he knew how important it was to support the troops in Wau. Eventually we were into the final home stretch. As we landed back in Port Moresby I remarked to one of my crewmembers, "Well that's one way of spending a pleasant Sunday afternoon," to which he replied, "Is it Sunday today?"

I then settled down to write up my story about Wau, and handed it into the censors as usual. Once more though, I found myself in the middle of a great deal of trouble, and the next thing that happened was that I was called in front of a General Jennings. He said, "You've been to Wau! Didn't you read the directive?" I said, "What directive?" Apparently the "Directive" had been stuck up on the bulletin board for a couple of days, and it said that no correspondents were allowed into the Wau area. General Jennings said that he would have to report the incident, which led to me being expelled from New Guinea. I was told that I had to be at an air transport base the next morning at 5 o'clock to fly down to Brisbane, where I had to report to the director of public relations to learn exactly what my expulsion entailed.

I went down the next morning to get my flight, but no sooner had I boarded the plane then the order came for everyone to get off. Apparently the Japanese were attacking the north of New Guinea, in the Bismarck Sea area. I didn't see the point in hanging around, so I managed to get myself onto one of the B25s that was leaving to fight the Japanese over the Bismarck Sea. This proved to be quite a successful operation in which the Japanese were defeated. When we got back I had a very good story to report, thanks to General Jennings, and once again I went to the transport centre ready to fly down to Brisbane.

One of the first things I did when I got there was to sit down and write my story of the Bismarck Sea Battle. Brydon Taves and another United Press man had by this time gotten themselves a little office, where I sat down with my typewriter, wrote my story and then sent it off. As it turned out I was the only correspondent to get the story out. The irony of this was that I would not have gotten the story if I hadn't received the expulsion!

I then went down to see the director of public relations, a Brigadier Errol Knox, later to become Sir Errol Knox, who in peacetime was a newspaper proprietor. He was in full sympathy with any newspaperman who had gotten into trouble for pursuing a good story. However, he was a Brigadier and had to obey orders the same as anyone else, so all he could do was to shake his head, and undertake to find out exactly what was to become of me.

After this I managed to get myself an aeroplane ride down to Melbourne, and was tremendously happy to join up again with Marie and Pat. Marie was teaching in a school in Melbourne, and Pat was on a break from Tintern, a boarding school she had been attending. One memento that I bought back with me was a crayon portrait that the official war artist Bill Dargie had drawn of me. He later became Sir William Dargie, and painted the official Australian portrait of the Queen. The picture that he created of me took approximately twenty-nine minutes to complete, and I am very proud of it.

Christmas 1942 was far more enjoyable than the previous one in Singapore. However, it was not long afterwards that I was told to get back to New Guinea, and no further mention was made of my previous expulsion. The war in New Guinea was now moving forward with a great rapidity. It was clear that the Australian and American forces were gradually getting the upper hand, and that the Japanese were slowly but surely being driven out of the island.

Harold outside a more established United Press office in New Guinea.
Author collection

CHAPTER FOURTEEN

The War in New Guinea, Hans Christian Anderson, and General MacArthur

One of the biggest problems to the Allied forces was a disease called *scrub-typhus*, which was similar to malaria, and was caused mainly by mosquitoes or other insects. The American forces in particular imposed very severe restrictions on their troops. They were never allowed to expose any body parts and had to wear long sleeve shirts, gloves, and nets hanging over their helmets to protect their faces. There were also strict orders that nobody should expose themselves during daylight hours.

One day when Gibson and I were driving around in a jeep, we were stopped by some American military police. I was wearing a pair of khaki shorts and a short-sleeve shirt, and was told by the police that they would report me for this breach of regulations, something that I had no idea even existed until that point. I had to appear in front of a Colonel Julius Blank, who was a medical officer and had been sent out to the Far East by Washington to specifically investigate the effects of *scrub-typhus* and malaria on the troops. He was very interested in me, and the fact that I was able to drive around with parts of my body uncovered and yet not fall victim to these diseases. After thorough examination and investigation, the only conclusion that could be drawn was that I had spent so much time in this climate that my body had become immune. I was quite an object of curiosity for him.

Once more I took the opportunity to accompany American aircrews on their bombing missions, to see how the war was progressing from the air. On one occasion I went up in a Liberator bomber named *Roarin' Rosie* that was being piloted by a John Mufich. He was leading a squadron of medium heavy bombers, with the plan of unloading eighty tons of explosives and carrying out some low-level strafing of troop concentrations and installations in the Lae area of New Guinea. Though the Allied forces were now starting to get the upper hand, on the ground, the Japanese troops were proving very difficult move back, and required continuous air attacks.

Our journey on the way to the target area was largely uneventful, as air supremacy was now starting to be achieved. Once we reached Lae, though, some Japanese Zeros attempted to intercept us, but our P38 fighters that had been covering the squadron managed to see them off quite easily before the Zeros could inflict any damage on us. I had the opportunity on this particular mission to position myself between the two waist gunners, which a year ago would have been a dangerous area of the craft to stand in, as it was so exposed, but was now quite safe. It also gave me the opportunity of using my binoculars to view the Salamaua area, close to Lae, and to see how the war had developed. We circled around the area about three times at a height of about five thousand feet. We knew that Allied ground forces were within a mile of our target, and so great care was going to be needed with the accuracy of our attack.

Mufich flew over the Salamaua Peninsula that joins the North Papuan coast with a threadlike isthmus, which I remembered from before as being thickly wooded with palm trees. It was now, however, thinned out to just a few skeleton-like trunks, which was due to the repeated Allied bombings. The airstrips at Salamaua were completely pockmarked with bomb craters, and I was unable to count how many there were as they were so numerous. The red-topped buildings throughout the area had been completely gutted, and Japanese bombers and fighters were strewn all over the place. Despite all of this destruction, there were still areas where the Japanese held strong with ground forces dug well in.

On our right wing I could see the Liberator named *Yankee Doodle Dandy* release a full load of heavy explosives on the troop concentrations, which were situated in a wooded area to the right of the Salamaua Isthmus. Some of the ground had not seen sunshine for thousands of years, but now the continual explosions had churned it up, leaving great tree trunks uprooted from the ground. We then unloaded eight thousand pounders into the target area, and the detonations were so great that they reverberated throughout our plane. We then swung out to sea again, leaving our target behind us, and as I looked through my binoculars I could study the black smoke and red flames that we left in our wake.

At the same time over Lae, Liberators approached targets in relays from different directions, with our P38s actively scouring the thick clouds in the skies above for any Zeros that might be lingering with the intent of causing trouble. I could see a single Zero far off in the distance as Mufich approached the Lae area, apparently making it's way back to base after a dogfight. With my binoculars I could also see red flames leaping from wharf side installations, and there were great columns of thick black smoke that rose about a thousand feet in the sky. The retreating Zero had obviously been unsuccessful in trying to defend the area; I could see from five thousand feet plenty of evidence of the damage that had been left by our squadron's attacks.

I could also see the Japanese and Allied position in the Mount Tambu area, where the enemy cunningly took advantage of every piece of jungle cover that remained. On the home run my binoculars once or twice also revealed Allied positions, showing Australians gazing up and waving as bomber flights zoomed towards base after completing their job of "softening" the Japanese resistance. The whole experience was fascinating as I was able to get a great overall picture of what was happening in this intense war; it was exactly the reason why I had not wanted the United Press to withdraw me from New Guinea.

Another mission that I went on was in the company of a Universal cameraman named Earl Crochett. We went up in a Liberator bomber called *Connell's Special*, piloted by a Lieutenant Colonel Arthur Rogers, on our way to Humbolt Bay off the north coast of New Guinea. Once more there was little air opposition from the Japanese as we made our way across the Owen Stanley Mountains at high altitude. Again the mood was quite relaxed until we began to reach the target area, when the excitement increased as we descended to three thousand feet in search of enemy shipping.

Before long we sighted an enemy freighter approximately thirty miles from the Wewak area. We unloaded five hundred pounds of bombs onto it, which landed on it's deck with a resounding explosion, and as we passed over it I turned around and could see smoke and an oil slick spreading out from the stricken craft. Crochett had been precariously crouching down on the catwalk that divided the bomb bay doors, shooting snapshots of the bombs all the way on their descent to the target. We now turned back in preparation for a second run, as the heavy calibre machine guns aboard the ship blazed away at us. Undeterred though, we let more of the bombs go, which this time fell just short of the starboard bow, but which rocked it quite violently. Some of our load had been fitted with small white parachutes, and I watched with Crochett as they spread out over the target. Even though we were able to see the crew of the craft jumping overboard, the anti-aircraft gun kept blazing away and the tracers from it flew directly underneath us.

The bomb bay doors were now closed as we started to prepare for our third run over the target, and this time we swooped right down as the altimeter first registered seven, then five, and then three hundred feet, and all our guns were blazing. We were passing now over a distance not much higher than the masthead, and skip bombs had been dispatched that Crochett was able to photograph as they entered the freighter's rear. We then turned and banked steeply, and prepared for the long journey home across the Owen Stanley mountain range once more.

I was delighted to meet up once more in New Guinea with my old friend Shanty O'Neil, with whom I had been on bombing missions a year earlier when I was first stationed in Port Moresby. I was lucky enough to accompany him again on a mission over Wau, this time in a B25 Mitchell Bomber, which was carrying three hundred pound bombs and armed with hundreds of rounds of ammunition for low-level strafing. So I rendezvoused with other members of the squadron just before dawn one day. All the weather reports stated that conditions would be favourable over the mountainous territory we were due to cross, which was a relief as I knew from previous experience that this was extremely difficult terrain to navigate.

As we approached our target the sky seemed to be filled with all types of craft. P38 and P39 fighters were weaving into formation above and below us, while B24 engines roared at a higher altitude, circling as they took up formation so they would be in place over their specific target section. Shanty circled four times over Wau, awaiting the "green light" to be signalled for an attack on the target area. Suddenly the command came squawking through the phones, "Here we go!"

In formation we roared downwards, way out over the Salamaua Peninsula, then circled for the formation to be picked up again before turning inland to the river mouth that marked the entrance to a steep ravine, a thickly wooded area on either side leading towards the target area. As we approached the coast I saw B24s dropping heavy bombs, which exploded far above the treetops with a vivid flash, spreading plumes of black smoke. Shanty twisted and turned the craft up into the ravine, and then cried to his co-pilot "bombs away!" The co-pilot flicked some small red switches on the front panel, which flickered a number of red lights, as Shanty took the plane into the steepest dive with all guns pouring tracers into the thick woodland. From all sides I saw Mitchell bombers pouring heavy calibre incendiary explosive shells into the area.

The whole business took less than about three minutes, after which Shanty then pulled the bomber into a steep climb over the sharp peaked craggy rocks. Looking back I saw the thick black smoke shrouding the entire target area. The feeling among the crew was that the mission had been a success. "Jeeze! It would be a miracle if any Japanese are still alive and kicking in that area," one of them said, as the squadron started to make its way home. I must say that the whole experience was very exhilarating, and that bombing from a B24 was a completely different proposition from what I had experienced before.

Shanty O'Neil flew over six hundred combat hours, and received almost every decoration available to him in the American Air Force. In recognition of this he was due to be relieved from New Guinea, and sent on a long leave back to the USA. To mark the occasion the American Air Force laid on a dinner for him, which was quite a feat really, as in New Guinea most of the food needed to be improvised. They made spaghetti using the grease guns from their aircraft, and cooked it with meatballs, all of which really made it a tremendous treat. It was all dressed with flaked cheese, and made a very happy occasion.

Then a tragic thing happened. Shanty O'Neil, who was rather excited amidst all the celebrations, went out to the kitchen to get a drink of water from the icebox. On top of the icebox were some yellow flakes that he thought were the same flaked cheese we had on our dinner, and so he took a handful of them and put it in his mouth. It was only then that he found that it was not flaked cheese after all, but a very powerful disinfectant that the Americans call lye, and this gave him some fearful internal damage. The last I saw of Shanty was of him being taken away in an ambulance, and I think he had to undergo some extensive surgery when he returned to America.

What made the achievements of the Allied Air Forces in New Guinea and Australia even more notable was that during the whole of the conflict they did not necessarily have the best aircraft or support. I reached this conclusion from listening to their conversations at the airbases and also by witnessing firsthand some of the points they were making. There were concerted efforts to supply the airmen with an adequate number of craft in their mission to halt the Japanese advance towards Australia, but these were not always backed up with the necessary supply of spares, ground support or adequately trained pilots. In the opinion of the pilots, the strategy of only providing large numbers of aircraft without this type of support was a futile exercise, and in some instances posed a bigger threat to them than the Japanese themselves. I personally knew of one mission where twenty-five Liberators were due to be employed, but only sixteen took off, due to minor defects in the remaining number of craft.

The airmen would also site problems in the allocation of aircraft, which were not suitable for the job they were intended to do. One example of this was in the way in which heavy bombers were being utilised for low-level attacks, which really needed the power of diving attack bombers. Their opinions were backed up by surveys of heavy bombing losses in the northeast and northwest sectors of the Pacific conflict, which showed that the fewest losses were under conditions where bombers were being used for their intended purpose at high altitudes. Using such large planes at low altitudes provided the enemy with a sizeable target that could not easily be manipulated to avoid their attacks. These types of operation really demand the attributes of a medium attack bomber like that of the B26, which I had seen myself in action over Rabaul at heights of just seventy-five feet. Outside of this, other losses were often from faulty take-offs and navigational problems.

The use of fighter planes was also something that they questioned. The

Spitfire that had been so successfully used in the Battle of Britain had also been utilised in protecting Darwin from enemy attacks. The pilots contested the appropriateness of this—the Spitfire may have proven effective over the short distances of the English Channel, but could be left vulnerable when having to cover the larger area of the Timor Sea. The Japanese realised this and used a tactic of specifically targeting Spitfires, using their best pilots in planes that could exploit the Spitfire's vulnerability over long-range distances. The danger in this situation could be increased if an inexperienced young Spitfire pilot got carried away during a dogfight. In the pilot's opinion, the P38 was better suited for the defence of Darwin.

Pilots also rated the effectiveness of the P39 *Airacobra*, and labelled it the "baby B17." Their views were backed up by research that showed statistically that the smallest number of pilot casualties occurred while operating a P39. Pilots who flew this craft and then survived a crash landing all bore a distinctive v-shaped scar on their forehead, which was caused by them coming into contact with the gun sight on impact with the ground. I witnessed a P39 crash landing, which was a horrendous sight—the wings were ripped off, propeller blades were hurled in all directions and its engine was torn out. Though afterwards, the pilot emerged with nothing more than the distinctive v-shaped cut, which airmen described as being the "sign of the P39."

Back on the war front in the jungle, the Australians were still slogging their way on foot across the Owen Stanley Mountains to Kokoda, where the Japanese where still thought to be firmly entrenched. On my travels one day, I came across a little United States Air Force unit who were making reconnaissance flights in light aircraft known as "hedge hoppers" across the Owen Stanley Mountains at very low levels. I managed to join one of the crews that were flying over to Kokoda, which at the time was still supposedly being held by the Japanese. When we arrived there though, the enemy was nowhere in sight, so we stayed there for three or four hours and raised the American flag.

We then flew back again to Port Moresby, and I wrote a story about the incident that caused a great deal of attention, especially in Australia. The main thing of interest was that we had managed to fly to Kokoda without any interruption, whereas the Australians were flogging their way through the jungle, anticipating meeting with the enemy at some point

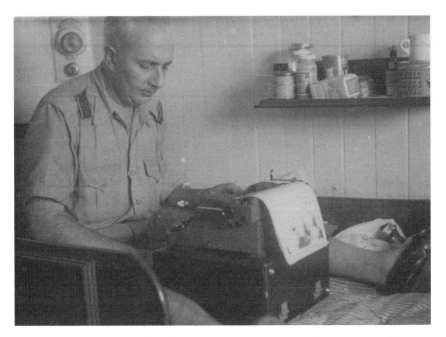

In the field—Harold at his typewriter prepares another report ready
for inspection of the censor. *Author collection*

during their mission. Marie sent me a cutting of my story that had been
printed in *The Melbourne Herald,* Sir Keith Murdoch's newspaper. This
incident had highlighted two very different approaches to the war.

The next bit of the war that I got mixed up in was in the Buna, Gona
and Sanananda area, and it was the first time that I had really been involved
in any coverage of the conflict on the ground. I would never want to live
through an experience like that again, and it really was a grisly business. It
was one of the final attempts to try and push the Japanese out of New
Guinea, and the Australian and American forces met with fierce Japanese
resistance whose troops seemed to be determined to fight to the death.
They were literally dug in within the area, and in some instances needed
to be blasted out of the ground.

Even when they were apparently wounded, the Japanese would be in
a fighting mood. Enemy troops that were supposedly injured would plead
with Allied troops, begging for water, and then promptly shoot any kindly
natured soldier with a concealed firearm if they stopped to help them. Even

the genuinely wounded would attempt to bite the thumbs off the stretcher bearers while they were being taken to hospital. The Japanese who were captured were found to have far lighter packs to carry than the Allied troops. The contents tended to favour weaponry and medicine, with more reliance being put on the enemy soldier's ability in finding food in the jungle, as opposed to carrying their own supplies.

One place where the fighting was particularly tough was in an area near the Tambu Bay that became known as "Roosevelt's Ridge." It was considered to be one of the most important strategic positions along the approach to Salamaua, as it provided a good vantage point and was very difficult to capture. The American troops here, though, were making steady progress, and gained more and more advantage the higher up the ridge they got—the Japanese started to loose sight of them because the Americans were quite literally hidden beneath their noses.

In spite of this the Japanese were still well and truly dug in, and continued their combat by rolling hand grenades down the ridge onto the approaching troops, which made for extremely uncomfortable conditions. Not only did the US troops have to deal with the inhospitable environment while climbing up the ridge to reach the enemy, they also had to contest with the prospect of grenades being dropped in a haphazard fashion from above their heads. Some of the troops who I spoke to about this conflict re-christened the area as "Son-of-a-Bitch Ridge," as they became so exasperated not only with the jungle conditions, but also with the stubborn Japanese resistance. They explained to me that the jungle rains were unrelenting; even when they stopped there was no respite as the raindrops continued to drip down from the jungle foliage. When they managed to reach some of the enemy fox holds, they would then drop a grenade into them, thinking they had cleared an area of Japanese troops. However, more enemy forces would later appear, and like the experience of those Australians I had met at Wau, it seemed that the Japanese must have had quite an intricate system of interconnecting trenches into which they could retreat to avoid the explosions. Though despite all these difficulties, the spirit amongst the Americans did not drop, and they kept launching attacks and encountering the Japanese in some of the bloodiest circumstances.

While in the jungle we were constantly living in about four inches of mud, as much of the area was near the coast and very swampy. The terrain and weather were unbelievable, and at times I honestly thought that our position was beyond being desperate, as even the experienced Australian soldiers were finding it difficult. Along the Sanananda and Kokoda Roads the ground conditions varied from dense jungle to marshland, and the soldiers were sunk waist deep in water as a result of several days of rain that caused streams to overflow. The Japanese foxholes and pillboxes were of an elementary design, made from local logs and mud, and connected together by crawl trenches. Enemy soldiers that were captured were mostly found to be starved, malaria ridden, and suffering from dysentery. The state they were in was typified on one occasion when blood transfusions were needed. Six prisoners were selected as donors, who would have normally produced six pints of blood, but it was only possible to extract half that amount from these worn out bodies.

In spite of these terrible conditions, the most positive thing to prevail was the comradeship that existed between both Australian and American soldiers. The battlefield also produced some amazing stories, one of which I remember in particular involved a Lieutenant Richards. He had led a group in an attack on the Japanese, but they were halted after making fifteen yards, and it appeared that Richards had been shot during the attack. A sergeant within the group reported that Richards had gone down under enemy fire. Though several attempts were made to retrieve his body, they were unsuccessful, being thwarted by enemy machine gun fire. All seemed to be lost. When nightfall came, once more the rain started to fall heavily, and amazingly the downpour seemed to have the effect of reviving Richards. He managed to make his way back to his command post, where they would have been less surprised to see a Japanese soldier.

Amidst all the terror of the conflict there was the occasional respite, and on one occasion I attended a race meeting that was held at an advanced base near the front. It was, I suppose, also a measure as to how confident the Allies were of defeating the Japanese, as all of this took place pretty much right under the enemies nose. The race meeting was organised to celebrate Independence Day on July 4th 1943, and there were seventeen events in all, which included horse, mule and pony races, tug of war, and relay races. All of this went on while fighters and bombers roared over our heads on their way to combat, but those who were left on the ground were

Harold writes his report in the thick of the New Guinea jungle. He is supporting his writing pad on his one good leg, while his stiff right leg is laid out straight. *Author collection*

more interested in placing their bets, which ranged from five shillings to ten Australian pounds.

Hundreds of pounds must have changed hands in total, and the activity around everywhere was frenetic. Mounts included those from the British Cavalry, which the Japanese had captured in Singapore, and were then retaken by the Australians around Buna and Sanananda. The track officials rode around in battered up door-less late model Fords that had also been seized from the Japanese. Lightweight carts, called silkies, had been made using the seats taken from the cockpits of downed Japanese Zeros. The race goers were all arriving in jeeps, bomb trucks, and gasoline wagons. Racing attire included American camouflaged jungle suits, Aussie slouch hats, and airmen fur-lined boots. The starting point for the race was a discarded airplane wing, and the finishing post was marked by a log that also doubled as a stand for the judges. The Australians were victorious in the tug of war against the American Air Corps team, who jokingly protested later that they had been robbed of the title. All of this was overseen by a group of puzzled looking natives, who probably wondered why everyone was running around in the mid-day sun.

Both Japanese and Allied forces were unaware that, while they fought against each other along the Kokoda Track, the Japanese efforts were being sabotaged by a group of Papuan naives. I found this out from talking to one of the natives called Fredrick Boski, from New Hanover in New Guinea, who had been enslaved by the Japanese. He was able to convey his story to me as he had received some education, on and off, for five years, and had also worked in an operating theatre of a local hospital that had exposed him to the English language. When the Japanese invaded they had rounded up many natives, and Boski had been amongst these people. Not all of the natives were captured, and the only reason why Boski was caught was because his own departure was delayed as he had been helping others to escape. The Japanese had forced Boski to act as a liaison between themselves and the natives, and to round up all of the headmen from the villages, who in turn were told to select the strongest of their men from their communities. What was unknown at the time was that these natives were then to be used as labourers and baggage handlers in the Japanese troop efforts to cross over the Kokoda trail and reach Port Moresby.

The natives had all been loaded onto a steamer with the Japanese

Allied troops take refreshments while gathered round the bonnet of Harold's jeep in New Guinea. Harold is second row, far left. *Author collection*

soldiers and horses at Rabaul harbour in August 1942, and thought the destination for their journey would be Blanche Bay. Though instead of cruising south, where all the steamers usually went for Salamaua, they turned northwards and then to the west. As night fell the natives considered hatching an escape plan, but were fearful of the repercussions that might befall them and the villages they had left behind. Any thoughts they had of escape were soon dispelled when a storm rose up, and the seas were so rough that many of the Japanese and natives were taken ill with seasickness. Gradually the storm died out, and at dawn they steamed on. Their journey lasted for another two days, as the route needed to be changed once more because of the presence of Australian ships in the area.

Eventually they reached what Boski later found out to be Gona. Australian planes passed overhead, but did not attack; Boski thought that was due to them being able to see that the boat contained mainly natives. The natives were pushed off onto launches by the Japanese, and then taken ashore where they straight away started their journey, which first took them up the Gona track.

Each native was made to carry a pack that weighed in the region of eighty pounds, and had to follow the Japanese troops who had horses and firearms. After two hours of walking, the natives were allowed some rest, and this was pretty much the pattern of things each day. They all rested for the night before continuing their journey the next day. The Japanese thought that they were well in control of the natives as the trek continued, but little did they know that the natives were already finding ways to sabotage operations. When they were on the track that went over the Owen Stanley, the natives would throw food supplies into the bushes when they were not being watched, and make small holes in the rice sacks so that the contents would leek out. Boski also told me how they would deliberately leave supplies behind, and when they were asked where the supplies had gone, they would quite innocently say that they had forgotten to bring it with them from the last staging post.

When food supplies became very low the Japanese would ask the natives about which berries and vegetation in the forest they would be able to eat. The natives would recommend anything that they knew to be highly poisonous, which the Japanese then ate with disastrous results. The irate Japanese troops would then beat them with either the flat side of their bayonets, or local saplings. Nevertheless, the Japanese were quite optimistic that they would eventually reach Port Moresby. The natives, on the other hand, knew that eventually their path would make it unsuitable for the horses. As the horses began to struggle, the Japanese troops would hand back their packs for the natives to carry, and if any of the natives refused or struggled, the Japanese would just beat them and leave them by the roadside without food or medication. In spite of this, the natives would continue in their efforts to halt the Japanese progress, and talked to each other about their situation using secret codes that the Japanese did not understand. For instance, they would refer to the Australians as "long fellow men."

The natives spent about fifty days in the jungle being forced to support the Japanese. It was when they had reached a place called Naoro, which was only about thirty miles to Port Moresby, that the advance was halted due to some very heavy fighting. The natives were told to go back to the last staging post to get further supplies. Boski realised that the fighting was near, as he constantly heard the sound of guns being fired. When they returned they were told that they were all going to have to move back, and from that point they continued to move further back each day. The Japanese told the natives that this was only temporary, that fresh soldiers would soon be coming as reinforcements, and that the plan to capture Port Moresby would soon succeed.

As time drew on and food supplies became scarcer, the natives lived on wild edible spinach and food from local gardens. Further retreats followed until they were at the Kokoda Trail, where they made camp again for a few days. They then left Kokoda sometime in November, passed Oivi, and camped a few miles from Kumusi River. The Japanese then crossed the river in boats and left quite a lot of the natives behind. Boski and some of his fellows decided that this was their moment, and swam across the river. From there he made his way to back to Gona, where he spent a few days living on taro (a type of root vegetable) and coconuts with other natives who had also escaped. They were then surprised to see a party of Japanese coming from an inland track, with apparently half of their party having already been killed.

On another day, Boski had gone out for a walk around Gona when he saw more soldiers. He hid in a bush because he was not sure whether they were Australians or Japanese; Japanese would often rob the natives, taking any belongings they might have. As they came nearer he could see that they were Australians, so he went to meet them and tell them his story. They picked Boski and four other natives to go with them to their camp, where they gave them food. Boski stayed with the Australians up to January 1943, helping to translate the pidgin English spoken by the natives who were escaping from the Japanese, which then gave the Allied troops valuable information about enemy movements in the area.

In the middle of my time in the jungle I got a cable over an army land wire from the United Press in New York, asking me to write what they called "a close-up profile" of General MacArthur at the front. This made me feel very angry, because I looked around at what the soldiers had to do and the conditions they had to live in, yet I was being asked to write about General MacArthur. I hadn't even seen him since I had been there, though I had heard that he had moved up to Port Moresby where he was living in a house previously occupied by a former Australian Military Governor. In my anger I sent a simple terse reply, saying, "You better get Hans Christian Anderson to write this one." I then had a reply from a Colonel Diller, who was one of General MacArthur's Chief Press Officers, asking me to get back to Port Moresby as soon as possible.

After my experiences in the jungle I was only too glad to get back to Port Moresby, and when I arrived I had to go and see Colonel Diller and a General Willoughby, who was the chief in charge of General MacArthur's Press Division. They both received me very cordially, and asked me about my message that said that Hans Anderson should write the story. I explained to them that Hans Christian Anderson was good at writing fairy tales, and so would be better suited to conjuring up some make-believe story. They listened attentively to what I had to say, and then said, "Oh yes, come on Hal! You know what New York wants. They want a piece on the General up in New Guinea." As a result, a breakfast meeting was arranged for me one morning with General MacArthur, and I was told I would be able to have an exclusive interview.

Our meeting was arranged for 8 o'clock the next day, and I promptly arrived for my appointment at his house. In front was a veranda with some cane furniture on it, so I sat myself down and waited for the General's arrival. Eventually he came along in a black silk kimono, with a gold dragon on the back. When he approached me I struggled to my feet, but he pushed me back into the chair and told me to remain seated. He sat himself down beside me, and then said, "I've heard a lot about you. Old submarine man eh?" Then he launched into a long talk about people who served in submarines, and said that they were the "Queen of the service." It was quite a long time before we actually got around to talking about the current conflict, and even when we did I found him to be very elusive in our discussions.

The General would regularly go off on tangents; he talked about Hannibal crossing the Alps, Alexander the Great, and even about General Alexander who at that time was having great trouble in commanding the Allied troops in North Africa. In fact, he managed to talk about everything apart from the topic of the war in New Guinea. Despite that, I came away from the interview and faithfully wrote down every detail—about the cane furniture, the black kimono, the golden dragon, what we had for breakfast and Hannibal crossing the Alps. It was of no surprise to me that none of the story was ever printed.

CHAPTER FIFTEEN

Lae Landings

I t was now approaching September 1943, and the next part of the war that I was involved with was an amphibious landing craft attack at a place called Lae, which is about halfway up the northeastern coast of New Guinea. It involved a large number of craft, called Landing Craft Tanks (LCTs), which were sailed across the Pacific from San Francisco and down to Brisbane where they were given minor re-fits. The operation was fairly big, which I think was part of MacArthur's so-called "leap-frogging" operations along the coast of islands in the South Pacific.

On September 1st, I was among a group of correspondents who boarded a C47 Douglas troop carrier plane that was on its way to New Guinea, in the first stage of what we had been told was to be the single biggest assault operation that there had been anywhere in the South Pacific area. After landing on a very muddy landing strip, I got a sense of the scale of the operation being planned, as there were more Australian soldiers than I had ever seen before in one place. Floundering in and out of trucks and sliding down slippery planks, I tried to keep up with the troops, who made their way in single file down to the waterside where the Landing Ship Tanks (LSTs)—a large craft used for hauling and launching the LCTs—were waiting for us with what appeared to be great gaping jaws.

With our exact destination still unknown, an Australian general explained that security was the strongest part of the whole operation, and that "we hope to catch the Japs with their honourable pants down." With this news the soldiers filed aboard the LSTs, laden down with all the necessary equipment needed for jungle warfare, which included the inevitable billycan. Those men were the heroes of the desert, and did not lack in enthusiasm, believing that the Italians and Germans were far harder opponents than the Japanese. One of them commented to me, "The Jap isn't as good a soldier as the 'Jerry,' in fact he isn't any better than the 'Eyeti' as far as I can see. The only thing I hope is that the little bastards are there in strength wherever we land. We want to polish them off straight away without the trouble of chasing them through the hills. Maybe then we shall have a Christmas at home for the first time in four years."

I waded through about two feet of water and boarded one of the LSTs, which was quite a struggle with a stiff leg, as the ramp leading up to the craft was set at a forty-five degree angle and was very slippery. Managing to wedge myself in between the Aussie soldiers for support, with my feet already sopping wet—which one of my comrades told me was fine as long they did not get cold as well—I managed to get onboard. I considered his observation as someone then cried out, "All aboard for the Skylark! Next stop Tokyo." We then set sail for our destination, still unknown to us, but with the certain objective to defeat the Japanese.

On September 2nd we were somewhere between Lae and Finschaven. It turned out that our vessel was carrying more than twice her maximum capacity, with both American and Australian troops onboard. As a result, the amount of cabin space available was limited, and some of the Australians who could not be allocated bunks camped on deck, making improvised tents from tarpaulins. I was invited to share a cabin with an engineer lieutenant called Michael Baughman Gill, who was from Miami, Florida.

On the table in his cabin was a photograph of his wife and two-year-old daughter Janice. He told me that he once assisted the United Press Miami bureau during the 1935 hurricanes. "There isn't much glamour about these vessels," he observed. "Boys aboard somehow feel they are forgotten, but many of them don't realise the important part they play in this war. I don't think they realise what a gigantic job they've got before them in this area, but I do know they'll do the job well even though they are brand new sailors."

To my surprise I was able to help Gill out with a problem he had with the steering gear on the landing craft. These vessels were driven by massive diesel machines that needed a lot of hydraulics to work the big ramp at the end of the boat and also the steering gear. During the journey it broke down, and Gill was full of dismay, as it meant that it would now take us five days to get to Lae; plus, we would need to resort to hand steering to keep station with the rest of the fleet. He and the chief mechanic were studying the blueprints of this steering gear, trying to find the fault, when just out of curiosity I looked over their shoulders at the plans. Suddenly I found my mind going back to the time I spent on the K22 submarine, when there had also been trouble with the steering gear. Laid out in front of me in the blueprints was the same type of machinery, and I asked Gill if he would let me take a look at the engines. Initially he was taken aback

Harold, back row, fourth from left, with other correspondents waiting to board a Douglas C47 troop carrier plane in New Guinea. *Author collection*

by my suggestion, but became more enthusiastic after I explained to him my background; he readily agreed, especially given the desperate nature of the situation.

Gill took me down to the engine room, and when we got there the engines were just as I had imagined them, with two rams and big springs for the steering gear to turn either to port or starboard. I knew exactly where to put my finger on the problem and asked Gill for a spanner. Within ten minutes I had managed to put the trouble right, leaving Gill completely amazed. "Good Lord!" he said, "A bloody correspondent has put the steering gear right!"

In the morning we had corned beef hash with two fried eggs sunny-side up after what was a sound night's sleep. The convoy was now steaming within sight of land, and repeatedly changing course and altering formation. It was a tricky business keeping a tight formation in these cumbersome crafts, and they tended to drift sideways with the wind and current. Our skipper said that on their voyage from the United States, some of these vessels drifted as much as forty miles off course each day. "In this part of the world, though, reefs are more dangerous to us than the Japanese. Handling these babies is a skipper's nightmare. But we always get where we want to—by guess and by God," he said.

Some of the Australian officers had now started to hold conferences around large-scale maps that were spread out over the mess room tables. Every platoon and every company commander was given detailed instructions, and the men were briefed on where exactly they would be landing. Drizzly rain did not perturb the camping Aussies, who were sprawling everywhere on deck. Wagers were made as to when they would return to Victoria and New South Wales, Queensland and West Australia. "Home for Christmas," said one—"Which Christmas?" came back the laughing question. The entire convoy spent the afternoon testing ack-ack and machine guns, which periodically relieved the monotony of our journey. The tests also gave us a foretaste of what was to come, and few of us onboard were of the opinion that this mission would be in any way a walkover.

Everyone was then issued with a lifebelt, and lookouts started checking everywhere for the presence of submarines. I could feel now the tension among the troops was starting to increase, as they sensed that the time was drawing nearer when they would be called into battle. Any small talk and "leg-pulling" that had been taking place amongst them began to dwindle, and instead their attentions were given to a much concentrated cleaning of guns, adjusting of equipment and discarding of unessential items. We were still a fair distance away from our objective, but the soldiers had to start getting themselves ready in good time, because from now on they could only make any necessary preparations in daylight hours, as no deck lights would be allowed once nightfall arrived.

The next day our fleet had grown, and now included six more LCTs, six destroyers and some ocean-going tugs. We anchored somewhere off the coast, and two submarine chasers came alongside us for fresh water, which they had been short of for some days. We had ample to spare, as Gill was disposing of all excess ballast in order to increase buoyancy of our craft in readiness for running ashore on the beachhead twelve miles east of Lae. Thousands of gallons of fresh water were pumped overboard, and I could see that there would now be many showerless days in front of us, which was not a prospect I particularly relished, as the heat between decks was really oppressive. As the day drew on the weather became even more sweltering, with a great scorching sun unrelenting above us in an otherwise empty blue sky. The water from the hoses actually boiled in the morning on the deck plates, and the steel sides of Gills lower bunk were almost unbearable to touch. Even the ink in my typewriter ribbon went soggy, which had the effect of blurring the letters as if they were blotted. Probably the coolest people aboard were the Australians in their tarpaulin tents, but anyone trying to get any sleep between decks found it pretty much impossible.

General Quarters were sounded twice during the day, and Australian troops manned their Bofor ack-acks as two planes flew over our heads at high altitude. There was even less chatter amongst the soldiers now, and the process of cleaning guns and checking equipment, once more, intensified. The troops had been told now that they would be landing at Lae, and I overheard the fleet surgeon confirm to the captain that they were ready with plenty of stretchers and everything needed to take care of burns. Company commanders were still poring over maps, pencilling notes and making crosses against unknown gun positions. Our troops were due to be landing on "Red Beach," while others had been allocated to "White Beach." One of the captains remarked, "I reckon ours will be pretty red by the time we have finished."

Our chief signalman, Ulan, had seventeen years service, and told me, "six months ago I swam ashore from the sunken Chicago, in the Battle of Rennell Island, but I shall walk ashore from this baby." He was the only veteran sailor in the entire flotilla. One of the yeomen, who was in his forties, was affectionately nicknamed "Pop" by his comrades, but he wasn't a veteran. In fact, the crew were made up from all walks of life, and were for the most part amateur sailors but doing a seamanlike job. Ulan told me that it was harder to handle a fleet of LSTs than a fleet of battleships. The irony of it all was that as sailors, most of their time concentrated on ways of keeping craft off the rocks, whereas in the LSTs, they have to find the best way of running them aground.

Early in the afternoon the fleet got into battle formation, with ocean-going tugs moving out on our wings, along with destroyers and sub chasers, while the LSTs and destroyers lined up abreast and astern in the centre. P38s were now flying overhead, and amongst the troops there was now open talk about the job to be undertaken. "Got to walk a bloody long way after we get ashore. I'd sooner go right in where the artillery is than footslog through the swamps," one remarked. Gill told me not to expect much sleep that night as it was the last stage before we started moving towards our target, and that we would all have to be "on our toes."

On September 4th the first landing was made, and Allied troops went ashore in considerable strength at the beachhead, twelve miles east of Lae. At 5:24 am there were red flares from the shore to indicate that the first landings had been effective, and momentarily the starlit sky was illuminated. We had been at General Quarters since 4:00 am, and waited nervously for our time to come. The sound of guns could be heard all around, and the blasts from them were also indicated by a series of intermittent flashes. Our destroyers steamed inshore to provide cover for the first small craft landings, and there was a smell of cordite after a heavy pounding of the Japanese positions. The LSTs now formed into a single column and then steamed straight onto the shore.

A group of planes up above alerted our anti-aircraft crews, but it was a false alarm as they only proved to be some of our P40s. The Australian troops then started to fasten their equipment, and fell into line ready for the elevator to take them to the landing deck. There were now more anti-aircraft puffs billowing up into the air, which had been prompted by reports that some Japanese Zeros were now approaching. At 7:20 am the troops started to descend the elevator, and the bow doors were then opened. The troops streamed out onto the beach, which was already thronged with their comrades swarming in all directions like ants. In the morning sunlight it was possible to see the wire meshed landing strips that had been laid down by American amphibious engineers in the second wave of landings, and over these, jeeps and tractors crawled in a long line, laden with every conceivable supply item.

Most of the jeeps were piled so high with supplies that it was barely possible to see the driver behind the wheel. Among the convoy were many bulldozers, which had already been tearing a path through the jungle that fringed the beach. Australian troops were filing into the various tracks that had been made, with different units being distinguished by their banner. There was again, briefly, some consternation as Zeros appeared on the port side, but they soon made their way off inshore at high altitude under the ack-ack fire from several of our ships.

We braced ourselves again as another group of planes were sighted coming over the mountain ranges, but once again this was a false alarm as they were identified as Allied craft. Our relief, though, was only short lived, as it became apparent that Japanese medium bombers were in hot pursuit of them, and they swooped in low over our heads. Again our ships put up a thick burst of anti-aircraft fire, but couldn't prevent some light bombs being unloaded and scoring a direct hit on one of the LCTs, which was quickly set on fire. Then another craft, further along the beach to the east, was also hit by some cannon fire. Several groups of Allied planes were overhead, and a formation of B17s flew over from the direction of Lae. After this, bombs were heard exploding, and their reverberations could be felt aboard our LST.

Whenever our planes went overhead the ground forces cheered their efforts in ridding the sky from enemy attacks. American engineers had already begun digging slit trenches in anticipation of further enemy attacks, while others had busily started to erect anti-aircraft guns. In amongst all of this frantic activity, I was amazed to find PFC William Pipelow covered in sweat and blood, apparently oblivious to the surroundings, as his only interest was in demolishing a can of peaches that had fallen from a split packing case of supplies. A nearby Australian private called over to him,

"Good on yah yank, don't let the bloody Jap interfere with yer tucker."

The landing and unloading of stores and supplies proceeded at a break-neck pace. Everybody seemed to find a place for everything, and all the stores were rapidly concealed and dispersed within the jungle. Occasionally the troops cast an anxious eye towards the sky, but throughout the rest of the operation it was only Allied planes that now flew over.

The LCI on the beach was still burning, and so our LST lowered its ramp and ran ashore, rigging up fire hoses in order to fight the fire. They managed to extinguish the fire, but unfortunately fourteen casualties had already been reported and at least four others killed. The ramp was then raised, and it pulled out from the shore to resume our formation in the fleet, with Buna being the next destination. It was now about two o'clock, and General Quarters were sounded once more and the crew closed up for action stations. Planes had been reported straight ahead, and anti-aircraft fire could be seen now in the far distance. The destroyers in the fleet constantly encircled the LST convoy, which from time to time had scattered out of formation. We heard that two more LSTs had been hit in the approach to Lae, inflicting further casualties amongst our comrades.

Red Cross staff patched up the casualties that were being stretchered aboard our craft, while a chaplain and doctors carefully scrutinised the wounded. Foghorns were sounded for the return aboard, so I clambered back up the slippery ramp into the LST. On board a doctor treated casualties on the loading tank deck, those who had ailments including a variety of fractures, lacerations and shrapnel wounds needing urgent blood plasma transfusions. The medical staff laboured under trying conditions late into the night, attending the wounded, but all of them seemed to make satisfactory recoveries. Overall, commanders felt that given the size of the operation, the casualties had been quite small, and that the day's operation had been the most important so far anywhere in the South Pacific.

The following day I found out that two of our convoy had been bombed and beached further up the coast. I had very little time to write any stories while dodging the frenetic activity on board, and so returned to Lae with the next convoy. On our way we were attacked by two Japanese Zeros that dived in from a high altitude and dropped two light bombs three hundred yards off our port side. Once more, the reverberations of the attacks could be felt on board, and the destroyers in our fleet fired several rounds of anti-aircraft fire in return and managed to see them off.

We then received official notification that the troops in our initial landing had now achieved their initial objective, which apparently was to reach a position across the Bulu River. This was six miles west of the landing beach, and was the position that had originally been bombed by B25s during the first action of the operation on 4th September. The general consensus of opinion was cautionary though, as it was expected that more opposition would be met the further inland the troops progressed.

I journeyed back and forth over the next two days with convoys between Buna and Lae, as I felt that it was the best way to spend my time; the troops who had gone ashore would still be making a pathway by flogging their way through the swamps and jungle. I went on a number of the operations with amphibious craft, along with several other correspondents. These operations were in the main quite successful, except for times when there was a breakdown in intelligence communications; also, a little flotilla of craft that were making landings on various parts of the New Guinea coast were mistakenly bombed by American airplanes.

They were not very severe attacks, but on one occasion Geoffrey Reading, an Australian correspondent, and myself, had to jump over the side and swim for shore from our particular landing craft. Barney Darnton of the *New York Times* was, however, killed in the incident, which was very upsetting for me, as I had spent much time with him over the past year. I kept Barney Danton's typewriter, an old Remington with a big "D" stuck on the lid, as a memory of him and our time together in New Guinea for many years afterwards.

On 7th September I went ashore and into the jungle to find out how the troops were progressing. In spite of the repeated dive-bombing and low-level strafing by the Japanese Zeros, I found that the Allies were actually making steady progress with the establishment of a complete rear supply base that was within a good distance from Lae. Since their initial landing, the assault troops had so far encountered minimum air and land opposition, with the brunt of the operation falling upon the engineers and various supply units. However, conditions did prove to be tough, which was not only due to the difficult terrain but also to occasional nuisance attacks from the Japanese dive-bombers. There were countless tales of courage from the troops, most of whom were experiencing their first action. At times the engineers could only make progress with the building of roads while under the cover provided by the pitch darkness of night. The enemy planes could at times play havoc, but as soon as they disappeared and the ack-ack subsided, the determined muddy and bloodstained engineers once more resumed their work and repaired any damage that had been caused.

Up in front of us a long column of trucks and jeeps trailed their way further inland, as I sloshed my way along the corduroy trail to the press corps jungle camp in sodden clothes. I repeatedly received many kind offers from Australian troops to carry my pack. They had seen that I was affiliated with the American forces, and were keen to repay the efforts of the American engineers in building the trails through the jungle. "The Yanks do everything they can for us and we want to do something for you fellers. Bigod if it wasn't for the American Navy we wouldn't be here and now it's the Yankee engineers who are making it easier for us to get at the bloody Jap," one of them commented. Another who landed with an LCI and met with the Japanese air opposition told me how the Americans had run a landing craft ashore into the teeth of an enemy dive-bomber, which had been attacking the Australian troops.

The conflict was relentless though, and on the previous day Japanese Zeros had carried out low-level strafing in two separate raids, making two passes each time. In the afternoon, medium bombers pattern-bombed the beach and dispersal areas, which had caused slight damage and a number of casualties. Again in the evening the bombers returned and bombed the road area, just before the start of torrential rain that swamped the press corps camp. We received some unconfirmed reports later that three Zeros and one bomber had been shot down on the beach by American anti-aircraft fire.

The following day was the first peaceful one since the mission had started. I shared the Press Corps camp with twelve other correspondents, and around us we could still hear the sound of Australian artillery shelling in the Lae area. Throughout the day American planes patrolled the area, covering the unending movement forward to the Bunga River, which was the foremost Australian position that had been reached without much opposition. Late in the previous night Japanese bombers had been zooming above, and explosions could be heard in the far distance to the west of us—

but since this was the only raid for twenty-four hours, it indicated to us that the enemy air strength was starting to wane considerably.

Living in the jungle presented many different types of personal nuisance, in addition to the anxiety of the occasional Japanese air raids. Visibility was limited to small patches of blue between the treetops, and at night there was a pitch-blackness that seemed to envelop everything. When enemy bombers did fly overhead, even the myriad of crickets and insects in the jungle were hushed, as if the animal life were joining in with the camped troops listening to the awesome roar of the aircraft. When there were flashes of tropical lightning, all the waiting watchers flinched; this would be followed by the first explosions of anti-aircraft fire, leaving us all prone on the ground digging into the jungle mud. There was also a chance of Japanese troops infiltrating our camp, so the perimeter to our camp was strengthened following reports that there had been enemy patrols in the area. The danger was sometimes increased in the darkness of the jungle, as it could become filled with suspicious sounds and shadows. Occasionally, trigger-happy sentries managed to shoot at their comrades by mistake.

The jungle camp was very basic, and less than comfortable. We draped mosquito nets from Liana vines, and then spread a groundsheet out on the sodden earth among the ants and leeches. In the darkness of night you lay prone on the ground, using your pack for a pillow, listening to the noises of the jungle. If the rain came you had to pull the ground sheet over the top of yourself, but in spite of these feeble attempts you still ended up getting drenched. Getting any sleep was therefore extremely difficult, but after a number of successive nights eventually exhaustion got the better of you. One night I slept soundly uncovered through four hours of torrential rain, and when I awoke I felt like a submariner, as I was lying in about four inches of liquid mud. The entire contents of my alleged waterproof pack were soaked, and so I decided to strip naked, draping everything over tree branches to dry out. I then spent the morning wallowing around in the Buso River trying to get myself clean.

Predominant among the insects that could be found in the jungle was a venomous looking red spider, which favoured habitation inside American-type steel helmets. There was also a species of purple lizard, which seemed friendly enough, but could give you a nasty shock when met unexpectedly in the darkness of night. Fireflies could sometimes take on the appearance of distant ack-ack flashes, and crickets made a ceaseless chatter and rustle which could also be mistaken for a rustling noise and potential nearby Japanese patrol. Needless to say we spent much of our time living on our nerves, terrified either by the inhabitants of the jungle or the occasional Japanese air attack.

Nevertheless, the Australian and American engineers continued to tear the forest to pieces on a daily basis, hewing logs for corduroy roads and making detours for streams of traffic hauling tractors and water wagons across country. Since the first landings it had been an engineer's war, and those brave men bore the brunt of the enemy assaults. They managed to harness a dynamo to the Buso River, the power from which would allow us to receive a broadcast communiqué. It was always interesting for us to read about what we were meant to be doing, because in the jungle, war coverage was sometimes limited to just the six feet of forestation which was around you.

The general consensus was, though, that the Japanese would make one last ditch effort to defend the immediate area of Lae, where there was no doubt that the more suicidal "fox-holed" defenders would once more be encountered. From the point of view of those of us on the ground, the most encouraging factor regarding the conflict so far had been the efficiency of the American air patrols, which official reports claimed had made a significant impact on the Japanese raiders. In addition to this, American fighters had destroyed the Japanese aircraft that were involved in the original attack on our troops during the initial landing. I spent 12 long days in the jungle with the troops before then returning once more to Port Moresby.

CHAPTER SIXTEEN

Passage to India

hen I got back to Port Moresby I had quite a surprise waiting for me. There was a very long telegram from the New York office, telling me that they now wanted me to go to India. This was the last thing that I wanted to do, and so I sent a reply back asking them why. There then followed a big interchange of cables and letters, and it was explained to me that a new headquarters was being formed by Lord Mountbatten in South East Asia, and that John Morris was in New Delhi and had requested that I join up with him.

The pressure was now on, and I returned to Australia to discuss the situation with Marie and whether it might be possible for us to take Pat with us. I started making enquiries but found it difficult to make the necessary arrangements, and encountered some of the most awful red tape that I had ever experienced in all my life. I do not think that there was another country in the world at that time which was so entangled with such bureaucracy as Australia. It was even expected that Marie should get an export licence so that she could take her wedding ring! Clearances were required from various government departments, and it put us right off the idea of travelling out together—I started to hope that there would be so much red tape that it would prevent me from going to India at all.

In spite of this, the New York office insisted that I go, and it was some-time towards the end of September 1943 that I finally set out for India on my own, by ship, and in the company of a Paramount News cameraman by the name of Martin Barnett. I think it took twenty-one days for that little ship to sail from Melbourne in Australia, to Colombo in Ceylon, and we had rough weather every inch of the way. We went right across what they call the "The Great Australian Bight" and around to Freemantle, where we stayed for twenty-four hours, and then across the Indian Ocean to Colombo. Every day the sea was rough, although the ship's crew were quite relieved by this, because they said that it lessened the danger of attack from any Japanese submarines, which were supposed to be swarming around that area.

I had to stay a couple of days in Colombo, and got a room in the Great Eastern Hotel. It was there that I made the acquaintance of a lanky American lieutenant colonel whose name was Kennedy. He attracted my attention because he was wearing a "bush whackers" hat like an Australian would, turned up at one side, which was an unusual choice for an American. Colonel Kennedy turned out to be a very nice fellow, and was working for a branch of the American army called JICA, which stands for Joint Intelligence Collecting Agency.

In the meantime Martin Barnett, the Paramount newsman, said that he was going to make his way up to India, by ship and rail, because he had so much camera equipment that he didn't want to fly. I had to go scurrying around Colombo to find out if there was any way of me flying up to New Delhi, and was very lucky to make the acquaintance of a Group Captain by the name of Harris. He was flying up to Bombay, and I asked him if I could get a flight with him. So one morning I was on an RAF plane that flew all the way up from Colombo to Bombay.

From Bombay I then needed to make my way to New Delhi, and was lucky enough to meet a man called Cambridge, who was one of the higher officials in Indian railways. He was flying to New Delhi on an Indian government plane, and said that he could give me a ride, during which he also pointed out various parts of the country to me. At New Delhi a car came to meet Mr. Cambridge, and he dropped me at the Marina Hotel where John Morris was staying. It was the first time I had seen him since Java in February 1942, and it was good to make his acquaintance again.

Whenever you book into a hotel in India, the first person to call on you is a man who wants to tell your fortune, and sure enough that is what happened to me. He came carrying a reference book with a list of names, from the Viceroy downwards, who were people he had apparently told fortunes for. He told me that I would not stay long in India, but one day I would return again. He told John Morris that he would also leave India soon, but he would never return.

I was, however, shocked by John Morris's appearance and demeanour, and he seemed to be really quite low. He had always been a rather flamboyant character, and very talkative, but now he seemed strangely quiet and withdrawn. In the ensuing days I found out that he had gotten himself into some very serious trouble by breaching sensitive censorship rules. A ship had been ferrying enemy prisoners for exchange with the Japanese, and had called at the Portuguese enclave of Goa. The correspondents had been allowed to go across to meet the ship carrying the prisoners of war, but only on the understanding that they not try to send messages from Goa. Everything had to be censored by the government of India, but John Morris had not obeyed the instruction and had attempted to send a message. Consequently he got himself into some very serious trouble, and to make matters worse this breach of rules seemed to have jeopardised his attempts to get a United Press service established in India.

I also met up with Daryl Berrigan, the young American who had joined me for a short time in Singapore, and then been sent across to Bangkok in Thailand. He told me how he had been driven out of Bangkok when the Japanese arrived, and then made his way to Burma, from where he had then made the long trek to India. It was quite a story, and I was very glad to meet up with him again. John Morris decided to fly off to Chungking because we had an office up there, and so suddenly I was left in charge of the New Delhi service.

I felt restless in New Delhi because nothing seemed to be happening, apart from the inevitable daily communiqués, which this time came from the Burma Front. The Japanese were gradually taking over the whole of that country, and things were becoming very grim. In addition to this, there was a large section of the Burmese people who had gone over to the Japanese side, as well as a pretty heavy section of the Indian National Army. As a result, the situation in India was very uneasy, and the anti-British feeling was running very high. The words, "Quit India!" would be written on the walls in numerous places. I wanted to escape from this country as soon as possible.

I tried to make some visits down to the Burma war front, but there seemed to be no proper facilities for the press there at all. In doing so I found myself in some very tricky situations—the Japanese were making great headway, against which we were offering little defence. Another battle was also being fought at a place called Kohima, right in the middle of a monsoon. It was more like an amphibious operation, with the troops swamped out, making the whole thing a terribly difficult operation.

I did not spend a great deal of time down on the Burma front; the entire situation there was very confusing and extremely dangerous. The Burma front was the longest battlefront in World War Two, being over two thousand miles long, and we had very little in the way of defence against the Japanese.

I soon made my way back to New Delhi where I had my first meeting with Lord Mountbatten, which for me was an unforgettable moment. It happened when a new American general was being appointed to the area, named General Wedemeyer. Lord Mountbatten gave a reception for his arrival, to which the press had all been invited. We had to dress ourselves up in our best uniforms—I appeared in an American uniform, but with my British war medals decorating it.

At the reception I found myself with Colonel Kennedy, who had also arrived in New Delhi by this time. We stood together talking, looking at the various personalities that were wandering about the room. One of them was General Joseph Stilwell, who was Mountbatten's Deputy Commander. He was an American with the nickname of "Vinegar Joe," and nobody really liked him that much. There was also a General Orde Wingate, who became famous for his involvement with the "Chindits"—troops that operated in Burma behind enemy lines.

When Mountbatten entered the room, he immediately spotted me with my British medals on. He came straight over and said, "How is it you're wearing those?" I said, "I won them Sir." He said, "I hope so, but where?" I said, "Royal Navy Sir," and he grinned all over his face. I said, "I do not expect you remember submarine H23 on which you did your training?" The next minute we were talking navy, and about the old days of submarines. He was interested to hear where I had been, and what I had been doing.

That was a great moment for me. I felt I had made contact with one of the men I had most admired in the whole world. One person who was impressed by my encounter with Lord Mountbatten and the stories I had to tell was Colonel Kennedy, of the Joint Intelligence Collecting Agency; he was amazed to find out that I had experienced so much. I did, however, have a bit of a brush-up with General Stilwell, who was the American Deputy Supreme Commander in South East Asia.

It seemed to me that General Stilwell wanted to fight the war in his own way. He had a lot of Chinese troops under his command that belonged to Chiang Kai-shek, and had his own method of combating the Japanese in Burma. General Stilwell's plan was to build what was to become known as the Ledo Road, to the centre of Burma, where he intended to get behind the Japanese lines and cut them in two. He was a great one for putting on the "rough and ready" act, and you always saw him in a sort of battle dress, but never a full general's uniform. I remember one day he gave a press conference at the Imperial Hotel in New Delhi, and it was during this press conference that he made reference to Lord Mountbatten as "Lord Louis Non-Combattant." This made me very furious, so I got up and walked out of the press conference. As I neared the door I heard General Stilwell say, "Whose that horse's arse?"

It was now 1944, and I found out that Admiral Sir Geoffrey Layton was at that time stationed in Colombo. I decided to go and see him, and he gave me the opportunity of getting my first "real" story from that area of the war. He shipped me aboard the aircraft carrier HMS *Illustrious*, which was going out on the first operation of the Eastern Fleet. American, French and Dutch ships were all involved, and they were going to strike at a place called Subang in the Dutch East Indies. It was good to feel like I was back as part of the navy again, and I think we were at sea for about nine days. I shared a cabin with a lieutenant commander in the Royal Navy Volunteer Reserve, called Michael Horden, who later became a famous actor on television, film and radio. He was a great character to share a cabin with, and was always full of fun.

I spent a lot of time in the Engine Room Artificer's mess and often went down to the engine room to get a taste once more of that part of navy life. The degree of information I was able to get about the war was largely restricted to the official communiqués; being on an aircraft carrier prevented me from seeing much of the action, and didn't make my reporting on the attack very satisfactory. However, I was the only correspondent who could claim to be involved with the operation, which provided me with an exclusive story, and that was all thanks to Admiral Sir Geoffrey Layton.

I stayed in the Galle Face Hotel in Colombo, where I remember all the guests sitting around the radio listening to the bulletin from London, which included my story about the HMS *Illustrious*. It was also about this time that my stiff leg became very inflamed—the problem seemed to be emanating around the deep flesh wound that I received from the flying tree splinter that had hit me during a Japanese air attack while I was in Malaya. It was so painful that I thought I better go and get it properly checked, and managed to find a civilian doctor who told me that I should go straight to bed. He fed me with "M and B" tablets, which I think were some sort of antibiotics, and they made me feel terribly miserable.

Colonel Kennedy became very concerned about my condition and sent for an American army doctor to see me, who made his own diagnosis of the problem. I told him about my stiff leg and flesh wound, and he said that I had gotten a "tropical ulcer." He said that he would have to get me into a hospital, and that I would have to be flown up to New Delhi where there were proper hospital facilities. The next thing I remember was being carted away and put on board an airplane, then admitted to an army hospital in New Delhi.

The Americans had very stringent treatment procedures for anything like a tropical ulcer. They put a lot of penicillin on it, then strapped it up, which made it hurt all the time. I was told to stay in bed and not get up at all, and that was how I spent Christmas—in a hospital bed in New Delhi. Eventually, when I got out of hospital, I found out that John Morris had flown home to America on leave, but also that he had put in an application to return to India. There seemed to be some difficulty with this, and New York asked me to speak to the appropriate authority in the Indian government to find out why there was a problem. To do this I had to see the Minister for External Affairs, Sir Olaf Caroe, who told me outright that they were not going to issue a permit for John Morris, presumably because of the previous trouble he had been in.

I informed New York of the decision, and not long after this I received some very tragic news. John Morris had been up to the United Press office on the 12th floor of The News Building, on East 42nd Street in New York, and had thrown himself off—he was extremely upset and frustrated about his difficulties in India. It was a very sad moment because I liked John Morris, who had given me my chance with the United Press.

Following the death of John Morris, I received a message from the United Press office in New York, saying that I was now being appointed the Far Eastern Manager. This changed my life completely, because it meant that I had to direct the movements of about a dozen correspondents in the South East Asia command. I had to do a lot of flying around the area, sometimes all the way from China and then down to Ceylon. We had correspondents on several sections of this massive war front, and it seemed to me that I was spending all my life flying around in airplanes. At times this could, however, be most exciting, and I remember making a journey over the Himalayas with the United States Air Force, which they called "going over the hump." It was a tremendous thrill to fly over that great "shimmering wall" which was the highest mountain range in the world.

The northern most point that I reached in China was Chun Ming. This was a very interesting experience because by this time the Chinese communists had announced their willingness to cooperate with the nationalist troops of Chiang Kai-shek in a common battle against the Japanese. I also travelled to Kabul in Afghanistan, which was a neutral country during World War Two. I found it to be a most extraordinary situation, with all the embassies of the belligerent countries operating in one ramshackle street, or boulevard, alongside one another. Another trip that I remember was to a place called Bangalore, where there was a big military command. I thought that I might be able to find some friends of Marie's, and went along to the military headquarters and asked to see the education officer. I met with a major who was the first person during my whole wartime experience to ask me for my credentials! This seemed amazing to me, as it had happened in a place that was far removed from any of the war fronts in Southeast Asia.

I then received a spate of bad news in quick succession. First, I heard that Brydon Taves, who was the United Press officer in General MacArthur's area, had been killed in an air crash in New Guinea, and also that another good friend, Frank Priest, a United Press photographer, had also been shot by a sniper. Another young fellow by the name of John Andrews, who was a correspondent in my area, was killed in a bomber out on a raid over Bangkok. It seemed that correspondents were getting killed all along the line, and it was time for Lord Mountbatten to shift his headquarters from New Delhi down to Ceylon. He set up new headquarters in a place called Kandy, and most of it was located in the botanical gardens that were nicknamed the "Garden of Eden."

It was while we were at these headquarters that I covered my second story involving sea action. I went to sea on a United States aircraft carrier called the *Saratoga*, which was part of the Eastern Fleet. It was quite a big operation meant to strike at a place called Sourabaya in the Dutch East Indies, which I was familiar with having been there before on a bombing mission from the Northern Territories of Australia. This time, though, I was able to leave the ship and take off in a dive bomber with an American commander called Joe Clifton, who had the nickname of "Jumpin' Joe Clifton." It was a terrifying experience, and I think for the whole time we were in the air we were in close combat. Jumpin' Joe really lived up to his name, plunging the aircraft down and then back up into the sky.

We managed to get back to the *Saratoga* safely, and as soon as we landed I went to my cabin to sit down, as the whole experience had shaken me up quite a bit. I badly needed a drink to steady my nerves, but unfortunately the American navy was "dry" and no liquor was allowed on board. So I tried to write my account of the trip with Jumpin' Joe Clifton, when a seaman named Peters arrived. He told me that the ship's padre wanted to see me, so I stopped my work and went to see him expecting to receive a sermon. When I got there he asked me to sit down, and then said, "Well Mr. Guard, I thought that you might need a spiritual uplift." He turned to the combination safe in his cabin and twiddled the little knob, and from it produced a bottle of bourbon whiskey, and poured me out a good big strong slug of it!

I had to leave the *Saratoga* in mid-ocean, as she was travelling round to the South West Pacific. I wished I had been able to stay, as one of the stops was Melbourne, which would have then allowed me to meet up with Marie and Pat. Jumpin' Joe Clifton promised that he would phone Marie on my behalf when they got there and tell her all about me. So I was flown off the *Saratoga*, and landed back on the British aircraft carrier HMS *Illustrious*. This was my second visit, and I was very glad to meet up with some very old friends again, including Michael Horden. We made our way quite safely to Colombo, from where I journeyed back to Lord Mountbatten's headquarters in Kandy. There was always a lot for me to do at the headquarters, as by this time we had almost a dozen correspondents spread out along the whole of the Burma war front. The war in Burma was taking a new turn with a new military leader in Burma, General Sir William Slim. He seemed to bring a tide of good fortune, and the Japanese were now gradually being repulsed.

During my time in India, I also got an insight into the country's future political development. I remember one occasion when I was with a friend called Stuart Emeny, who was a correspondent with the *London Daily Telegraph*. It was on a Sunday evening at a rather famous hotel in Old Delhi called the Maidens Hotel. We were having a meal when our attention was drawn to a very gaunt looking man with a shock of grey hair, who was wearing a long tight-fitting grey coat. He seemed to be gazing at us very intently, and was apparently on his own, so I went across to him to ask if he would like to join us.

We got into conversation with him, and learnt that his name was Mohamed Ali Gina, the leader of the Muslims in India. He then told us a story that at the time we thought was most improbable. He told us about his organisation's dreams of forming a country of their own, in a separate part of India. When India had ultimately received its independence from Britain, they were going to form this new nation that would be called Pakistan. It seemed to be such a far out dream at the time that Stuart Emney and I found it almost laughable. Unfortunately, Stuart Emney was killed not long after this when he was flying with Major General Orde Wingate, and their plane crashed killing them both.

I then learned that the American Air Force was flying planes from Colombo, in Ceylon, down to Perth in Australia. It was called the "longest hop," and was a distance of three thousand six hundred miles. I was determined one way or another to get a trip on one of these planes, so that I could fly down to Australia to be with Marie. It did not take too long to get permission, although the conditions for flying were very unusual. The planes would take off from Colombo and then almost immediately drop radio communication, as they had to pass straight over enemy territory. On a Sunday afternoon I took a flight on one of these planes, and was very surprised to find that I was the only passenger on board. Apparently two planes had taken off, and the other one was carrying three American generals. The flight lasted sixteen hours and was not unpleasant at all; I slept for much of the way, then finally arrived in Perth.

When the plane landed I was most surprised when an Australian officer opened the door, and told me that there was a car waiting for me. I was also informed that I would be staying in The Palace Hotel for the night, then flying onto Melbourne the following morning. I could not understand why I was being treated so well, but was of course very appreciative of the hospitality. The next morning, though, I got up to catch the plane, and a lot of young Australian officers were standing by the aircraft, waiting for me to get on the airplane first. We set off for Melbourne, and on the way we stopped off at an Australian airstrip and had a mid-morning breakfast. While we were walking back from the mess hall, I said to the pilot that I had never been treated so well, and for a war correspondent to be made such a fuss-of was really most unusual. "War correspondent!" he said, "we've got you down as a general!"

They had thought that I was a general who was meant to be travelling down from Perth to Melbourne. The airplane with the three generals in it had not made the trip, and had to make their way back to Colombo due to an engine fault. Of course they could not report anything by the radio, and since our airplane had kept on going to Perth it was assumed that I must then be a general. At Melbourne Airport there was a staff car to meet me, and I was then driven all the way home to Stratton Heights.

CHAPTER SEVENTEEN

The Fortune Teller Was Right

My luck did not continue much longer though, as I had not been back in Melbourne that long before I found out that I was in trouble with the United Press for having left my assigned area without permission. I admit that this was the wrong thing to do, but I had reached a point where I was totally exhausted from reporting on the war pretty much non-stop for three years. I had been to virtually every possible war front, on land, sea, and in the air, and felt that I needed to stop and get the stability from being at home for a while with my family.

However, I was soon receiving cables from New York, asking me about my actions, and they made it very clear that they wanted me to get back to India as soon as possible. Personally I thought that I was better off in Melbourne—I could get back to areas with which I was better acquainted and had so much success in the past. I made the point to them that the main offensive seemed to be coming from the South West Pacific, but all of my arguments proved to be fruitless.

At the same time I received a number of job offers, which although were quite tempting, I turned down as they did not fit with my future plans. One of them unexpectedly came from Sir Keith Murdoch, who invited Marie and I for Sunday lunch up at his country house in a district just outside of Melbourne. He sent a car to pick us up and take to his house, where we had a lovely lunch together with him and his wife. We all got on very well together, and it was not until after lunch that Sir Keith Murdoch suggested that I should stay in Australia, and sign a contract with him. I told him straight away, though, that my future sights were set on London as a place to settle and work.

The New York office was still pressing me to get back to India. They told me they were appointing a new Far Eastern manager, with whom they wanted me to work, whose name was Miles Vaughan. I had no inclination at all to return to India, as there was so much trouble and political unrest, so it was with great reluctance that I eventually agreed to go back. For my return, I took one of the few airplanes that had started to run from Perth to Colombo. The United Press paid for my flight, but it cost a terrific amount of money in those days—I think about three hundred and seventy-five pounds. So it was now sometime in October 1944 that I found myself back in India, which was quite in line with what that fortune teller had originally told me on my first visit. He had also sadly been correct in saying that John Morris would not return.

By this time our newly appointed Far Eastern manager, Miles Vaughan, should have arrived, but there was no sign of him in New Delhi. I learnt through word of mouth that he was in Calcutta, and so I flew there to meet him. I found him to be a short little man with a rasping voice. My visit to Calcutta at that time also coincided with the All India Newspaper Editors Conference that was meeting in The Great Eastern Hotel in Calcutta. So I seized that as an opportunity to circulate a letter between all of these editors to introduce our new Far Eastern manager on behalf of the United Press.

This turned out to be a very useful move, as Miles Vaughan soon made it known to me that his chief endeavour in India would be to sell the United Press service, rather than do any more war coverage. He also made it plain to me that I was to help spearhead a new promotion of the United Press service in India. This was quite a fearsome job, because I knew that for some years the United Press had been trying to get established here, but without much success. I made a proposal to Miles Vaughan that if I managed to get a service started in India, by selling it to the *Times of India*, which was the largest newspaper in the country, that he would promise me a transfer back to London. He said, "Boy if you sell to the *Times of India*, you get the top brick off the chimney! You can have anything you want!" That was enough incentive for me, and I was determined to succeed so that I could return home.

I told Miles Vaughan that I was going to Bombay, because that was the logical place to start a news service, as it was the cable head for India. In Bombay I booked into the Greens Hotel, which was a sort of adjunct to the best hotel in Bombay, the Taj Mahal. When I arrived there, the very first person that I talked to was an American by the name of Mike Chaflin, who was in the film distribution business. He was the most humorous character, bespectacled and slightly balding, with a very dry sense of humour. When I told him that I worked for the United Press we became friends straight away. Another person who I met was a chief petty officer in the American Navy, whose name was McNamany. He was in charge of a radio monitoring station that they had just established outside of Bombay. The Americans had a number of these stations in various parts of Asia, where they could pick up all the short wave broadcasts from almost anywhere in the world. This little chief PO, who I nicknamed "The Admiral," told me that they listened all the time to the United Press broadcasts from the United States. I mention these two people, because they both played a vital part in the programme that I followed in Bombay during the ensuing weeks.

A few days after arriving in Bombay, my best hopes were nearly shattered when I found out that our leading competitors in the United States, The Associated Press, had already established an office in Bombay, and worst of all it was in the building occupied by the *Times of India*. That seemed to doom any effort of mine to establish the United Press. I had to quickly find an office in which to establish ourselves, but after searching the city it seemed that almost every available space had been taken, by either the army, navy, or government agency. The Associated Press office in the *Times of India* building was a very tiny little room, but this had at least given them a start and a great advantage over us. I told Mike Chaflin about this situation, and he said, "Well boy, why don't you take a room in the Taj?" The Taj being the Taj Mahal Hotel, and together we went across to see the manager.

The Taj Mahal Hotel stands on the waterfront of Bombay, looking out over what is called the "Gateway of India," an archway built in red sand-stone right on the sea front. It has been the archway through which all of the rulers of India, including the British Emperors, had arrived when they first set foot on Indian soil. The Taj Mahal manager explained that every single room was booked, and that the only room still available was the Princess Suite. The Princess Suite was a suite of circular rooms built in a turret on one corner of the hotel, looking out on the gateway of India, and was most luxurious. It consisted of a separate sitting room, bedroom, and bathroom. The bath was sunk into the floor, with great big silver plated dolphins that gushed out torrents of water into a white alabaster bath. In the bedroom there was a circular divan, and mosquito nets ran up to the ceiling forming a sort of a regal throne. All these things frightened me off, as I assumed it would be too expensive, but Mike Chaflin persuaded me to take it. He said, "Take it boy, think big! Talk big! Get in here and you've got an address." So it was on the spur of the moment that I agreed to take the suite, and in November 1944 the United Press office was established in the Taj Mahal Hotel.

The next thing to think about was our communications. We had to get radio reception for our United Press newscasts from San Francisco and London, and I had no equipment at my disposal. I asked Miles Vaughan, who had by now arrived in New Delhi, to send me an assistant, and he very promptly sent me a young man by the name of John Hlavacek. He took up residence with me in the Taj Mahal Hotel, and together we scoured Bombay to get all the materials that we needed to get a news service started. None of these things were easy to obtain, and included: carbon paper; copy paper; a typewriter and above all, a radio receiver. We let this be known to the little American chief petty officer, and he got for us what was called a Hellschreiber Short Wave Receiver, which was very powerful.

John Hlavacek and I carried this between us up to the post master general in Bombay, and in no time at all we were receiving United Press broadcasts. Then we had to make an arrangement with the Indian Tele-graph to distribute the news over their landlines, so that it could be sent as far as New Delhi, Calcutta, Madras, and Ahmadabad. It seemed to me that anywhere in India was at least two thousand miles from anywhere else; it was no easy task to distribute a news service over such a vast area, and it took us some weeks to get it established. However, we eventually succeeded. The Indian Government would provide our radio reception over the receiver that had been given to us by the American CPO, which we would then collect from the post office in Bombay and bring back to the Taj Mahal Hotel, from where we would re-write it and distribute it to the various potential clients.

During Christmas 1944, I made my first contact with Sir Francis Lowe, who was the rather redoubtable editor of the *Times of India*. Sir Francis was very well respected in the newspaper world, and I sent him an invitation for him and his wife to join me in the Taj Mahal Hotel. He turned out to be a very nice gentleman, and his wife was terribly excited at being a guest in the Princess Room. They were most interested to hear about the United Press, Marie, and how we had left Singapore, and by the end of the evening we were all on very friendly terms.

A day or two later I went to see Sir Francis Lowe in his office, and put it to him fairly and squarely that United Press had promised me that if I was able to sell a news service to him, that I would be granted a transfer to London. For a moment or two he just sat there and looked at me, and then suddenly burst into a hearty laugh, and said, "Well that's a type of sales talk I never heard before!" He said that if I sent him a trial service, then he would see how it went. So I sent him a trial service of the United Press News for about three weeks, after which time he wrote me a letter to say that the *Times of India* would become a subscriber. The first part of my objective had then been achieved, and the United Press had gotten their first foothold into the Indian news service.

The United Press affairs were going ahead very well indeed, and I had another assistant sent to me called Stuart Hensley. I think it was sometime in early February 1945 that Miles Vaughan came to New Delhi and installed himself in the Greens Hotel with Stuart Hensley—there was no room for him in the Princess Suite, which was now a hive of activity as our service got underway. I anticipated that once we had sold to the *Times of India*, all the other English language newspapers would also want to take our service. It was now our task to distribute the service to other parts of India, which was a very difficult thing to do because the Indian posts and telegraphs were not always that reliable. In India, communications could be damaged by the extreme weather experienced in a monsoon, or even by a stray elephant knocking down the landlines. We made good progress though, and became well known in Bombay, and were even the subject of a feature in a weekly magazine called *Forum*.

One of the most interesting characters I came across during this time was an Indian called Jamnadas Dwarkadas. He was a huge man with grey hair cropped very short who wore a voluminous dhoti, which is an Indian robe of a pale beige colour. He came to the Taj Mahal Hotel and sat himself down on one of our low divans, and I was rather surprised that as he sat down a big fold of his dhoti seemed to hit the floor with a thump, and I wondered what it was that had hit the deck. Jamnadas Dwarkadas was one of the leading men on the Bombay Cotton Exchange, and the reason for his visit was that he wanted me to get him the opening quotation of the cotton price on the New York commodity market.

That was a job that I did not want to do. Because of the previous experience I had in Hong Kong, I knew what a tremendous effort it meant for the United Press. To get that one quotation meant that we would have to have a man on the floor at the New York Cotton Exchange, and as soon as the market opened he would have to phone in with the price to our New York office, who would then transmit it to San Francisco, who would then in turn transmit on our radio broadcast to Bombay. We would have to have someone there at the receiving station to then phone it in. The whole essence of the exercise was speed, and Mr. Jamnadas Dwakadas' main idea was to get this quotation first, which would mean an awful lot of money to him.

To try and put him off, I told him that it would cost a lot of money, and though I had no real idea how much, I came up with a random figure of at least ten thousand American dollars per month. To my astonishment he stooped down and groped in amongst his dhoti, and produced a great pile of one hundred rupee notes done up in rubber bands and put it on the table, which he said was a deposit. So we embarked on this rather difficult task of getting the opening cotton price for Mr. Jamnadas Dwarkadas, and we were quite successful, though it was not easy. It meant that we had to break off in the middle of very important news bulletins just to get the figures. Mr. Jamnadas Dwarkadas was quite happy though, and continued to pay us ten thousand dollars per month for the service.

In April 1945 we managed to get a big coup for the United Press, and released the news of President Roosevelt's death before all the other news agencies. John Hlavacek and I were asleep in the Princess Room, when sometime after midnight the telephone rang, and on the other end of the line was the "Admiral," my American CPO contact. He said, "say we've got some big news for you. We've just been listing into the UP cast, President Roosevelt is dead." That was a shock, and my first action was to get John Hlavacek to call the *Times of India* to see if their paper had been completed for the morning press. I told him to pass the message on to hold the front page, and then in the meantime got down enough details to cover the full gist of the story. It was then that I had to get in touch with one of the military censors, Ross Parker, who was also living in the Taj at the time. I called him up, much to his annoyance, and asked if we could release the story, because it would be on the wire shortly, and he agreed.

I began talking then to the *Times of India* people, and they found, much to their consternation, that they didn't have an obituary for President Roosevelt. So I had to sit down and write an obit in the middle of the night. The work I had done with Swan, Culbertson and Fritz, the American stockbrokers in Hong Kong, came in very valuable, and I was able to describe everything that Roosevelt had done in instigating the "New Deal," and about all the various other things that he had done during his first and second terms as president. All these things came flooding back to me, and I was able to add a little more detail to it, such as that he was the first American president to fly in an aeroplane, and about his polio. From this I managed to put together a respectable obituary. In the meantime, John Hlavacek had gotten things organised, and we had a lot of messenger boys running round to all the newspapers in Bombay delivering the news of President Roosevelt's death. I am very proud to say that on the following day, nearly all the news in the *Times of India* was almost solidly United Press news, and most of it was written by Harold Guard.

I think that this sealed the fate of the Associated Press, our greatest American competitors in India, as they were not able to sell their service at all. It was a triumph for the United Press, and it was shortly after this that I got cables from our president Hugh Bailey, as well as Virgil Pinkley, the vice president in Europe, congratulating me on what Bailey called, "an historic coup." By this time we had gotten things pretty well "ironed-out," as far as the United Press was concerned, and I thought that it was time to remind Miles Vaughan of the promise he had made me.

I broached the subject with him and he tried to side step it, and said that we still had plenty to do. It was clear to me at this point that he was not going to keep his promise, which made me very angry as I felt that I had delivered my side of our bargain. So I started to make my own plans, and find a way back home to Britain in spite of Miles Vaughan's reluctance to recognise my achievements. To this day I do not remember exactly how it happened, but somehow I managed to get myself onto an RAF flying boat that was going to back to Britain on April 24th 1945.

I always remember a great feeling of apprehension as we approached home, as they announced in the airplane that we all had to have our vaccination and inoculation certificates ready for the immigration people to inspect. Although I had many vaccinations and inoculations, I did not have any certificates, and so I felt terribly nervous as we landed. I was wearing an American army uniform, and as we went through immigration, a young official saw me and said, "Well there's no need to ask you if you've been inoculated." He had mistaken me for an American, and so I just said "Sure thing buddy!" I managed to get through, and I was very relieved at last to be back home.

CHAPTER EIGHTEEN

Returning Home

The day after my return, the first thing that I needed to do was to let Marie know that I was in London, and also to present myself at the United Press offices at 30 Bouverie Street. Virgil Pinkley, the vice president, was away in Europe, and the office had been left in charge of man called Clifford Day, a long serving United Press man, who made me very welcome. He was very surprised by my arrival though, and asked me what I was going to do. I had scuttled out of my job in India without letting anyone know, and so it was left to Clifford Day to inform New York of my whereabouts.

I was told that in order to work in Europe I would have to be accredited as a war correspondent for the European theatre, as the war was not yet finished. To do this I had to go around to the various American and British headquarters in London to get all the necessary papers, and this process took me a couple of days. My thumbprints had to be taken, along with my photograph, and everyone seemed to be looking at me rather curiously, as I was dressed in a somewhat strange uniform for the European theatre. In South East Asia and the South West Pacific, the war correspondent's uniform being worn was quite different from those being worn in Europe, and I was the object of some curiosity. While getting my accreditation sorted out I also saw quite a bit of the city of London, and got an appreciation of the dreadful bombing that it experienced throughout the war.

The first notable event to happen after my arrival was VE Day, the end of the war in Europe, May 8th 1945. I remember wandering out of the office and walking up Fleet Street, and up The Strand into Trafalgar Square. There were hordes of people dancing and shouting and singing, but despite the celebrations and happy scenes, I found myself feeling sad and lonely. I had not shared the same experience as these people, and found it difficult to feel any connection with their joy, especially as I knew that in the Far East the war had not yet finished.

Back in the office I was busy once more, and one of the first jobs that I was given was to improve the communications for our service to India. I knew from experience that India had been suffering from poor radio reception, so I went to see the radio telecommunications people in London, who were very cooperative. After experimenting for a week or so, we found a medium wave radio band, which was ideal for India; although it was slow, it was reliable. The United Press staff christened this transmission as "GDB," which stood for "Guard's Dam Buster," something I found very amusing.

By this time Virgil Pinkley had arrived back in London, and I was very happy to meet him again. He was an extremely nice chap, and I sat with him for quite some time and told him all about my experiences in India. He understood why I would have been keen to get back to Britain, but told me that Miles Vaughan had been sending cables to New York recommending that I be fired from the United Press, because I had run out on my job. Virgil Pinkley was not in favour of this at all, and said that he was going to do everything that he could to dissuade New York from such action. This situation was, of course, terribly unsettling news for me, but was outweighed by hearing that Marie and Pat were to set sail for home and were due to arrive in June.

On 6th August 1945 we received some astounding news in the United Press office. I was sitting at the news desk when suddenly there was a news flash on a teleprinter from New York, saying that the United States had dropped an atom bomb on a place in Japan called Hiroshima. A girl sitting opposite me who worked for one of the sub-editors screamed out, "What does it mean?" Of course that was the question on nearly everyone's lips, as none of us had any real comprehension of what the atom bomb was. The messages from New York all anticipated that this would lead to an early surrender by the Japanese, though this did not happen until two or three days later when a second bomb was dropped on Nagasaki. An announcement by the Japanese then followed, saying that they were willing to surrender. So the World War was over, and I was asked to write a summary using my Far Eastern experience of the war against the Japanese, and what their surrender would mean.

However, Miles Vaughan was still pressing for my dismissal. Virgil Pinkley would have nothing to do with this at all, but wanted to demonstrate that some action had taken place in regards to my position. The only solution to the problem that he could think of was to send me to Prague in Czechoslovakia, to open up a new office for the United Press and demonstrate that I had been given a new task. I was disappointed by this decision, as Marie and I were by this time just starting to set up a new home in Streatham, but there was nothing I could do about it. So it was that I set off one morning for Prague, late in November 1945.

The whole business was made more complicated, as I had to take with me a huge Hellschreiber shortwave radio receiver that was in a wooden packing case. I was also carrying a package for a man called Walter Kolarz who worked in the United Press office, and who had escaped during the war and had come to London. His mother was still in Prague, and he asked if I would take her a Christmas parcel. So I set off one morning for Prague.

Virgil Pinkley had told me that I would be met in Prague by a United Press war correspondent by the name of Bill Disher, who was still in the Czech capital. The flight to Prague from London was anything but comfortable. I flew in a converted transport plane, and had to sit in what they called "bucket seats." I was lumbered with an extraordinary amount of luggage, including the large packing case containing a radio receiver, my own suitcase, a typewriter, and also a fairly large parcel that I had agreed to deliver to Walter Kolarz's mother. I began to wonder what would happen at the other end if there was nobody there to meet me, which I thought was quite probable, as there had been so many delays taking off due to the fog.

We eventually arrived in Prague, after not too comfortable a journey, in late afternoon. It was bitterly cold on the airfield at Prague, and the sky was dark, grey, and overcast. As I expected, there was nobody there to meet me, and I was dumped on the airfield in Prague with my array of luggage. Eventually Bill Disher arrived at the airport with a car, and piled me and all my baggage into it, and then drove me some miles into Prague.

Bill Disher was an extremely nice young fellow, extremely tall and very handsome, dressed in the uniform of an American war correspondent. He filled me in on the background of the situation in Prague as we drove into the city. From the things he had to tell me, I felt it wasn't a very encouraging outlook. He told me that he was engaged to a young Czech lady, and that her father had been a general in the Czechoslovakian army who had been forced to live more or less underground during the war years. They had acquired a big Mercedes motor car, and were saving every penny they could, hoping that one day they were going to be able to make a run for it from Czechoslovakia. That didn't really encourage me at all on my first visit to the country.

I didn't waste any time, though, in installing a United Press office in Prague. It wasn't a very difficult job. There were still some newspapers in operation, all very hungry for news, and the editors and staff of these newspapers were very welcoming to me. So my task wasn't too difficult, and we were able to recruit quite a number of local staff for the new United Press office. I forget the rate of exchange, but the Czech money was in Krowns, and there were about two thousand Krowns to the pound. The cost of renting an office and employing staff seemed to be extremely cheap, and our expenditure wasn't very high. We were also lucky in finding an expert radio operator, and in no time at all we had our Hellschreiber short wave receiver set up in our rented office in one of the big squares in Prague, and were soon receiving the United Press broadcasts. More than once, though, during those days in setting up the office, I encountered obstructions and annoying delays from government officials who were clearly being oppressed or directed by the Russians.

I enquired among the Czechoslovakian staff that we had working for us the whereabouts of Walter Kolarz's mother's house. It was then that I became aware of a strange atmosphere that seemed to overlay the whole city. None of the Czechs seemed to want to tell me where the house was, and none of them were prepared to take me there. Bill Disher didn't know exactly where it was either. Although he made enquiries, and did manage to find out where the house was located, he didn't seem ready to show me. He explained that if he did so, and was seen to be in contact with the mother of a Czech who had defected from the country several years before, that he could easily come under suspicion. It was an oppressive atmosphere, and there was something sinister about the whole life of the city. I suppose we people in England can't fully appreciate this, because we have never been occupied ourselves. The Germans had occupied Czechoslovakia for nearly seven years—they were now being threatened by a Russian occupation, and everybody was fearful.

I often felt like I was being watched, and remember going to a night club where all we did was sit at some rather bare little tables, and drank beer that tasted like it was made from onions. In the centre of the floor there was a circular platform on which a boy and girl on roller skates kept on revolving, and this went on for two or three hours. The entire time, I sat at a table near two Russian soldiers, who very ostensibly unholstered their guns and laid them on the table. I have no idea whether they were interested in me, but it is significant that they sat there as long as I did, and when I got up and moved off, they got up as well.

Nonetheless, I eventually met a Czechoslovakian by the name of Curka who had courage enough to direct me to the house of Walter Kolarz mother's house, which was in one of the residential outskirts of the city. I had to go alone though, which I did, and when I got there I met a sweet old lady who couldn't speak a word of English. She was dressed in a black frock, which was trimmed with lace, and she reminded me of "Whistler's Mother." I delivered the parcel to her, and she was highly delighted. I then made arrangements to get her out of Prague and on to London where she could be with Walter Kolarz. I can't tell you the exact details, in case others may be put in danger by doing so, but I can tell you that she went by barge all the way up to Amsterdam, and had to be hidden away the whole time. She eventually reached Walter in London early in 1946, and lived happily with him there for two years.

The time in Prague really seemed to drag. It was very cold, the food was unattractive and unpalatable, and I longed for a cup of tea—the coffee we drank tasted like it had been made from acorns! In my hotel they served what they called a continental breakfast, which consisted of a few crusts of bread and a tiny pot of jam, the taste of which I was uncertain. None of the food was very appetizing, and you couldn't get anything substantial.

As the days went by I became engrossed in finding an airplane to get back home for Christmas, which would be the first Christmas that Marie and Pat and I would have spent together since 1942. I was looking forward to getting back to our new house, and went to the airport and asked about flights. I was told there would be a flight leaving on 21st December, and so I got all my gear and gifts packed, and prepared to leave Czechoslovakia. By this time the United Press office in Prague was working well, and another American correspondent by the name of Sam Hales had been sent from London to take over as office manager. I was able to hand over to him an office in good working order, and was looking forward to returning to England for Christmas.

December 21st came, and I was out at the airport bright and early, in plenty of time for the flight, only to be told that it had been cancelled on account of fog. Prague is situated in an almost complete circle of mountains, and when it gets foggy it closes in over the city very densely, and flights do become very difficult to get. We were told to report on the following day, but again the flight was called off on account of fog. Again on the succeeding day, 23rd December, the same thing happened, and I was starting to think that I would have to prepare myself for spending Christmas in the very downcast city of Prague. I decided to make the best of the situation and bought a bottle of Slivovica. It is a Czechoslovakian or Balkan drink, a very raw sort of brandy made from plumbs, and sold in long slender bottles.

On the morning of 24th December, I went down to the lobby of the Hotel Adlon, put down my bottle of Slivovica and called for a glass, determined to drown my sorrows. Sitting at a table across from me was Peter Oxford, a young Royal Air Force officer who was looking as miserable as me. I called across to him, "You stuck here for Christmas?" He said, "Looks like it" so I said, "come on and help me with this." He got another glass and I poured him a big slug of Slivovica, and we both swallowed it and grimaced. It seemed, though, to give him an inspiration, and he said, "Have you got all your gear packed?" I said, "Yes I have," and he said, "well you stay here and get ready," and with that he was up and off. After about an hour he was back again, and he said, "Let's go!" Outside he had a jeep, and we drove out to the airport where there was a Royal Air Force transport plane. The fog was just as thick as ever, but this didn't deter Peter Oxford, who was a flight lieutenant and the pilot of this RAF transport airplane. So we piled everything aboard including ourselves, and we took off, right through the fog into brilliant sunlight all the way back to London.

After Christmas I went back to the United Press office in London and found that some significant changes had taken place. A lot of the United Press men who had been stationed all over Europe during the war were now returning to London. They included a lot of famous names, including: Richard Macmillan, who got the OBE for his coverage of the Normandy front during the D-day landings; Jan Yindric, who made a name for himself long before the war had started by reporting on Hitler's activities, from Munich through the invasion of Austria and Czechoslovakia; Tosty Russell who was very famous, and who broke the story about King Edward VIII's

Harold at his desk in the United Press London office after World War Two.
Author collection

romance with Mrs. Wallis Simpson; Ed Beatty, who had been taken prisoner by the Germans; and Walter Cronkite, who became one of the chief correspondents for Columbia's broadcasting system. In Fleet Street itself there were big names like Drew Middleton of the *New York Times*, and Joseph Harsh of the *Christian Science Monitor*, and I felt that I had suddenly been thrown feet first into the most competitive world that I had ever encountered. I might have been one of the "Big Four" in the South West Pacific, but in London I felt that I was one of the lower four hundred!

In 1946 I found out that General Percival, who commanded the troops in Singapore, had returned to Britain and was now retired and living at a place called Much Hadham in Hertfordshire. He had been completing his official dispatches on the events that had taken place in Singapore and Malaya, which the War Office had been withholding from publication by classifying them as "secret," and which had caused a great deal of controversy in Parliament and the press. Incidentally, when his dispatches were finally published in 1948, some of the value of the narrative was lost through the War Office declining to reproduce three sketch maps that General Percival had submitted. I wrote to General Percival asking if I could come and see him, and was delighted when I got an invitation for lunch at his home. So I travelled down by train, where he met me at the station and then drove me out to his house in the country, where his wife had prepared a lovely meal for us. After this we sat down and compared our experiences in Malaya and Singapore.

General Percival had actually served two periods of service in Malaya. The first one was in 1936 as a general staff officer at the headquarters for the Malaya Command, and his brief was to help develop the defences of Singapore Island. On this first spell of duty he told me that he was quickly able to see that the preparations for the defence of Singapore were inadequate, but there was little concern about this from the local population who seemed more concerned about the running of their businesses.

Like myself, General Percival had found that the Malaya Peninsula could be quite an inhospitable environment, but did not necessarily provide the impregnable natural defence to Singapore that many people envisaged. At this time, of course, the Japanese were increasing their influence in the area, and these matters, which I was able to corroborate through my own work, concerned Percival so much that he felt it necessary to record them in a report. I was interested to learn that a year later, when Percival finished his first tour of duty in Malaya, he had handed his report about the defence of Singapore into the War Office.

In spite of highlighting the deficiencies in Singapore's defence in his report, Percival found that the government was not responsive, and seemed to pin a great deal of faith in a plan that they already had, which was to have the troops already based in Malaya defend the island against any attack from the Japanese until the British fleet arrived. There were various aspects of this plan that appeared to be deficient: one was that Percival considered there to be insufficient numbers of troops in Malaya to defend the peninsula; also, the British fleet would take two or three weeks to get to Malaya and could be delayed by war in Europe.

It seemed to me that the government hoped that a war with Japan could be avoided completely, but this went completely against the evidence that Percival had gathered. I thought back to the reaction my own article had received in Singapore, when it was described by the authorities as being a canard, and could see how single-minded and flawed their belief had been. When Percival returned to Malaya in 1941, having been appointed General Officer in Command, the Japanese influence had increased in the area and the prospect of an attack became all the more real. Like myself, he was dismayed to find that there was little provision for any air cover. More aircraft had been provided but they were mainly older craft that would not necessarily be of any use in the modern battlefield. Percival also agreed with what Admiral Sir Geoffrey Layton had told me regarding the lack of naval defence, and deployment of the wrong types of vessel to fight the Japanese.

Since returning to Britain, the general had made it his main endeavour to challenge the official figures and statements that had been made on the defence of Singapore, and the proclamation that the defence of Singapore had been one of the most spectacular disasters to befall the British armed forces. He felt that some views had been put forward by commentators who had little first-hand knowledge of the conditions that existed in Malaya, and the decisions that needed to be made during the defence of Singapore Island were not made. One of his points was that the number of Allied troops defending the island had been overstated by the War Office; in fact Allied troops faced a greater quantity of Japanese soldiers, who were supported by a far superior air and naval force.

These were points that I could appreciate from having made numerous journeys up country into Malaya, both before and after the Japanese invasion. In fact, when faced with this superior force, the Allied troops' retreat had taken place over ten weeks, in very tough jungle conditions, without the support of a flotilla of ships to help with their evacuation, as had been the case in the three-week retreat from Dunkirk and Mons. Due also to poor communications and confusion, some units had become detached and lost. Circumstances were not helped by the apparent disgruntlement of some of the Indian regiments, who may have been affected by Japanese propaganda. Therefore, rather than being shameful, the resistance put up by the defending troops was truly heroic. Criticism of their efforts was an injustice that General Percival strongly felt needed correcting.

The troops were also ill prepared for defending the island, and this was in spite of the War Office knowing in advance that there was a threat of invasion from the north through the supposed impregnable jungle. As early as 1938, the GOC for Malaya at the time, Major General W.G.S. Dobbie, contacted the War Office and told them about the vulnerability of Singapore to attack from the north, and that the jungle did not provide a natural defence and was indeed passable. No action appeared to be taken regarding this warning, and I had seen for myself the ease with which troops could make their way through certain areas where forestation was not as thick.

Another thing that General Percival took issue with was the continual postponement of a plan to pre-emptively defend against any enemy movement from the north known as Operation Matador. This would have involved occupying southern Thailand, but the delay in implementing the operation seemed mainly for political reasons, and the desire to not provoke any unrest. It would appear, though, that this was more like wishful thinking, and hoping that any potential problems that might interfere with the commercial operations in the area would just go away. However, General Percival was certain that if Operation Matador had been swiftly implemented, the course of events that took place in the Malayan campaign could have been altered.

He gave me a lot of facts and figures, which I combined with material that I had gathered myself during my period in Singapore, and went back to the office to write about our meeting. I found General Percival to be a gentleman, and very scholarly in his appraisal of how the war was conducted in the Far East. However, the level of criticism that he used in refuting official statements and figures I thought was rather tame, and when I returned to London I wrote a very long story about all that had happened. Virgil Pinkley considered this to be important enough to have it copyrighted. The story refuted a lot of the statements that had been made by Winston Churchill, both during and after the fall of Singapore.

I feel very sad to relate that after I had finished my article, none of the London papers printed it, although it did get printed in the *Yorkshire Post* and in most of the newspapers in the Far East, including those in Singapore, Malaya, Hong Kong and above all, in Japan. It also led to a question in Parliament by a Mr. Dodds-Parker, a member of parliament, who asked Winston Churchill if he had read the dispatches by Harold Guard, correspondent of the United Press, regarding the campaign in Singapore and Malaya. Mr. Churchill replied that he had not read the dispatches himself, but from what he heard it would seem that Mr. Harold Guard would be better suited to a chair in Whitehall than a reportorial desk in the United Press.

CHAPTER NINETEEN

Post-War

I n 1947, life on Fleet Street was extremely busy, and for a time I was heavily involved with a project that the United Press had set up at the time called "The Executive News Service." It involved me travelling around Europe selling a specialised service to industrial clients, who wanted all types of information. This became quite a big operation until there was a complaint made to the British Board of Industry alleging industrial espionage had taken place. I also covered the breaking news of the independence of Burma, as well as the Royal wedding of Princess Elizabeth. I got involved with the London Olympics the following year, which was not something I felt best qualified to do with my stiff right leg. However, with the threat of being fired still hanging over my head, I was happy to still be in my job in whatever capacity, although as time drew on that problem seemed to gradually subside.

I learnt at this time from the admiralty that the British government had decided to demolish the island of Heligoland up in the North Sea, off the coast of Jutland. During World War Two the Germans had developed Heligoland into a marine base, with heavy batteries of big guns that were a continual menace in the North Sea. The British navy had been given the job of demolishing the base, and a number of British correspondents had been invited to go across to Germany for the occasion. I went up to Hull where I boarded a naval mine sweeper called HMS *Albercore,* and travelled across to Cuxhaven, which was a naval base in Germany used for operations in the demolition of Heligoland. There I met a lot of very interesting people, including Richard Dimbleby, who became famous as a BBC commentator and who also reported on the explosion of Heligoland from an aeroplane. The navy told me that 4,000 tons of explosives were going to be used to demolish the gigantic concrete submarine bunkers, pens and heavy gun batteries.

It was a large explosion, and though we were some miles away from the island, we felt the effect of the explosion, and also the huge tidal wave that followed it. The thing that intrigued me most about the operation was that I found out that the British and American governments had established a ring of listening posts, in various parts of Europe and the world, to listen to the effects of the explosion. This seemed to be such an elaborate operation for such a relatively minor explosion, until I later found out that this ring of seismographic stations had been set up not only to form a circle around Heligoland, but Russia as well. The establishment of these listening posts was a cover to listen for the explosion of Russia's atom bomb, which they knew was going to come at any time.

A lot of changes at the office were taking place, and a whole batch of new staff, mainly American, were brought in to replace all the famous names within the United Press. My position was now safe, and much to my surprise I was assigned to cover The United Nations Conference, due to be held in Paris in 1948. The main topic to be covered was the creation of the State of Israel, which was a subject I had no great knowledge of; I had to do quite a lot of research in advance of my journey. When I attended the conference I found that I came into contact with many interesting characters who were delegates from the African and Arabic states.

I met all sorts of interesting people from Algeria, Morocco, Iraq, Saudi Arabia, and Yemen. They were all fascinating people to talk to, because at that time they were the leaders of what could only be called rebellions in those nations. They were fighting for independence and the liberation of their countries from foreign domination. They used to tell me all about the developments in the Middle East, and the plans on the part of the Arabs to oppose the formation of the State of Israel. Gradually I began to get a better understanding of the issue, which was extremely complicated and still poses problems today. I do not think that it is unfair to say that the meeting of the United Nations was a non-event, and that nothing was settled.

I was delighted in 1949 to become reacquainted with a newspaper correspondent by the name of Patrick Maitland, who I had originally met in Australia and New Guinea. He was an amazing character, a member of a very ancient Scottish family who later on inherited an Earldom, giving him the title of the Earl of Lauderdale. He also had some very serious political ideas, and in the 1951 General Election he won a seat of Parliament for the North Lanark constituency.

One of Patrick Maitland's projects was to promote an idea that he and a group of other MPs had come up with, called the Commonwealth of Nations. The basic premise of this was to cease the British Commonwealth, and instead have a community of many nations, all of whom were prepared to collaborate with one another. The movement gained quite a lot of momentum during 1951 and 1952, and Patrick Maitland wrote a book about it called, *A Task For Giants*. I became very interested in the Commonwealth of Nations; I wrote many articles about it, and sought support for it from the many contacts I had made around the world.

I continued to carry out my job at the United Press, covering news stories such as the Festival of Britain and the death of King George VI in 1952. During this time I also began to get invitations from the Foreign Office for a series of "chats." I was not unfamiliar with the Foreign Office. Bob Scott, who had worked for the Ministry of Information in Malaya, worked there, and from time to time I had sought his help when covering news stories. He had been taken as a prisoner of war in Malaya, and remained there throughout the whole of the conflict. Afterwards, Bob Scott was involved in a lot of discussions and investigations at the Foreign Office about what had happened during the Pacific War. He told me some very interesting stories, and one that I remember in particular related to the sinking of the two British battleships, the *Prince of Wales* and *Repulse*.

They had been sunk not far from the Mersing area of Malaya, when they were on their way up the east coast of Malaya to Kota Bharu, where the Japanese landing was taking place. During this journey they got a signal from Singapore saying that there had been a landing further down the coast in the Mersing area. So the ships changed course, and it was during this manoeuvre that they were attacked with torpedoes from Japanese bombers that had been shadowing them. Further investigation into these circumstances showed that there had been no landing in the Mersing area at all, and that it had actually been a false alarm, caused by a buffalo straying onto the beach and setting off some land mines. A succession of explosions had lead to a signal being sent to Singapore reporting a landing, and this had then been passed onto the two ships telling them to change course. It could be said, I suppose, that the *Prince of Wales* and *Repulse* had been sunk by a water buffalo!

I was surprised, though, as to how much the people at the Foreign Office knew about me, and during my chats there, frequent reference was made to the news stories I had written, and to the people I had come into contact with at the United Nations in Paris from the Middle East. Eventually they made me a proposal—that I should visit a series of countries around the world, including those from the Middle East, Africa, and the Far East, to make an assessment of what was happening in them. For my journey the RAF would be at my service, to fly me to any point where they were able to go. I was very excited by the proposal, as it meant that I could go back and visit the places where I had worked during the war, including Hong Kong and Singapore. I went back to the United Press office to tell them, and they were keen that I take up the offer, as it would make a great story.

So I started to prepare for my journey, making sure that I had all the relevant documentation, passports, and visas. In February 1953 I was flown out to Malta to meet once more with Lord Mountbatten, who was now the NATO Commander in the Mediterranean. It was like meeting an old friend, as he had remembered me from our previous meeting in India. I talked at length with him about NATO, and what was happening in the various countries that I was to visit. He wanted me to talk to the people in these remote areas, and, as he put it, to "get into the skin" of them, as they may be important to NATO in the future.

From Malta I flew to Cyprus, and then onto Cairo where there seemed to be quite a lot of unrest. The country's leader at that time was General Neguib, but his leadership was under question and there seemed to be more support from the people for a man called Nasser. Everyone was talking about him; you couldn't even take a taxi without Nasser's picture displayed on the dashboard. I met with General Neguib, but he had very little to say, and didn't strike me as being a particularly powerful leader. It was also apparent to me that there were many American and Russian contractors in the country, all vying for contracts, in particular for the building of a great dam at a place called Aswan.

My next destination was Libya, and as I flew over the desert, the relics of the war were clearly visible below, with burnt-out tanks and the remains of guns, as well as other military equipment. I stayed in Benghazi, and once more I found there a growing feeling of unrest among the population. Oil had only just been discovered there, and it seemed to be at the centre of most of the conflict. The country's ageing king, King Idris, was under threat from many dissident factions that were looking to take over. I then flew into Sudan, and Khartoum, where arrangements had been made for me to meet with Sir James Robertson, the British Governor. Here the level of unrest was even more in evidence. As I travelled by car to meet him, there were hordes of rebels brandishing spears, which they occasionally banged against the side of the vehicle.

I stayed in Sudan for four days before making my way to Kenya, where there was a big RAF installation not far from Nairobi. The country was in the middle of a terrible uprising by the native Mau Mau, and I heard some terrible stories about the atrocities that were carried out by them in the jungle. I was taken on a military "sweep," as they called it, in the area, which was operating against the Mau Mau. In the army patrol that I was with I was given a Sten gun by a young officer who showed me how to fire short bursts from it. I warned him that newspapermen did not fire guns, and that I might not be much help to him in an emergency.

Our patrol went into some tall elephant grass, which was tall enough to obscure the view for many yards in all directions. Occasionally on our patrol I heard shouting and shots being fired, but I could not see a thing and it was only when the patrol was over that I discovered that they had captured about half a dozen Mau Mau fighters. They were fearsome looking people, with their foreheads deliberately caked with mud, and draped in animal skins.

From Kenya I then travelled to a place called Habanya, in Iraq, which I used as a base to make journeys out to the surrounding area. Most of the time it seemed there was trouble brewing. The problems were mainly caused by the disposing of many Palestinians from their homelands, which was a result of the creation of the State of Israel. The United States had come forward in an attempt to alleviate the problems of the Palestinians, with what they called a "Point Four Plan," designed to give them a lot of financial aid. In a meeting I had with General Sir John Bagot Glubb, commander of the Arab Legion, he told me that three out of every five dollars that was being given as aid to Palestine was being spent on administration. His exact words to me were, "The only thing that the American Point Four Programme had done for the Palestinians was to raise the standard of Bridge playing in Jordan."

I was also flown down to the Gulf of Aqaba, where stories were still being told of Lawrence of Arabia. Aqaba had been one of his strongholds when he was forming the Arab armies during the First World War, and there were rumours that there was a buried hoard of gold hidden somewhere in the region. While I was there, Air Force men would often go out with metal detectors in their spare time looking for this buried hoard of gold, but none of them, I think, were successful. I also visited Basra on the Persian Gulf, where a lot of American companies were drilling for oil. The city was obviously very militant, and it seemed that the prospecting of oil had aroused nationalism within this part of the country. In Baghdad there also seemed to be a lot of discontent, with young men parading around the city with banners proclaiming communist ideas. I was quite sure that the country was on the verge of a revolt.

My next stop was Aden, in Yemen, where the colonial secretary there told me of the problems they had been experiencing with some of the tribes in the northern territories. In an endeavour to improve relations they were keen to make contact with a character called the Sharif of Beihan, who was something of an unknown quantity. The colonial secretary was not sure if the Sharif was on the side of a rebellion, or whether he was in favour of remaining in what was known as the British protectorate. They thought that I might be able to help with this situation, as a newspaperman may present less of a threat by not being viewed with the same level of suspiciousness as officialdom would.

So it was that I went to meet with the Sharif of Beihan, along with a delegation of official representatives from the colonial office, and although he was, in appearance, quite a fearsome character, he seemed to take a liking to me. I spent many hours sitting on the floor of his palace partaking of his hospitality. Our conversation was translated by a young man called John Savage, and the entire time we were surrounded by the Sharif's tribesmen, who stood along the walls of the palace with piercing eyes and fang-like teeth. After what seemed to be many hours of conversation, the Sharif suddenly decided that he wanted me to be his blood brother. I was astounded by this request, and asked why, to which he replied, "Your hair is white, which shows that you have great knowledge. Your face is unlined which shows you have a young heart. You have a great wound in your leg, which shows you are a warrior. Therefore you are fit to be my blood brother!"

Meeting with the Sharif of Beihan. West Aden Protectorate and Wing Commander Forsythe is greeted by the Sharif prior to his meeting with Harold, when they became blood brothers. *United Press*

The rest of my journey through the Middle East took me to Bahrain, Kuwait, and the Red Sea area. After this I went onto Karachi in the newly formed country of Pakistan, which I had previously known under Indian rule. I found that everything had deteriorated under the new regime, and that there was terrible inflation. I only spent two days there before flying

Oil pipes being laid in the Middle East—the cause of much trouble, as Harold was to discover on his trip in 1953. *United Press*

Harold of Arabia—modelling an Arab headdress that was given to him during his travels through the Middle East. *Author collection*

onto Ceylon, where I was able to take a look at Colombo, and once more I was shocked at how dilapidated it had become. I looked forward to the next destination in my trip, which was Singapore.

After landing in Singapore, I was put through quite a lot of intense questioning from the authorities about the purpose of my visit. It was then that I got a really nice surprise. The RAF public relations officer, who was due to meet me at the airport, had brought with him Wee Kim Wee, the Singapore Chinese who I had employed when we first opened the United Press Office in December 1940. I had last seen Wee Kim Wee when I left Singapore in something of a hurry in February 1942, just as the Japanese were taking over the island. It was a great pleasure to meet with him again, and we had plenty to talk about.

He had a car and took me around to see some of the old familiar places. I went to see Marie's former quarters in the Alexandra Barracks, where I found little had visibly changed. I was told, though, that if I wanted to go to the Swimming Club that I could only do so as a guest, because Europeans were not allowed there alone. It seemed that the local population were starting to assert themselves, and that the British were no longer considered "top dogs." I was billeted at the RAF station in Changi, which had once been a dreaded place because it was there that the Japanese imprisoned most of the British troops in 1942. Wee Kim Wee told me that during the Japanese occupation, Johnny Fuji had contacted him, and together they went to find out if I had been captured. Of course they were unable to find me, and assumed that my getaway had been successful.

I took the opportunity of also travelling back up to Kuala Lumpur. At that time there was an "emergency" in Malaya, and for the past two years communist guerrillas had been travelling down into the jungle from the north, and the defence forces had been trying to force them out. I met with a General Sir Gerald Templar, who had agreed to meet with me as long as anything that he told me was off the record. When I met the general he gave me a long explanation about the difficulties the armed forces had experienced in getting rid of the guerrillas, but they were now getting the upper hand on their enemy after two years of tackling the problem.

It occurred to me that the size of the ground forces stationed in Malaya was as large as that which had fought in 1941, but they had the added advantage of support from the air and sea. Given that they had been unable to defeat their enemy, surely it vindicated the efforts of those who had fought there eleven years ago? I put it to the general that the criticism, which had been made of those who fought in the Malayan Campaign, had been harsh, given these facts, but he made no comment.

I also had my first-ever helicopter ride from Changi. I was taken up by a young naval pilot on a sortie into the Malayan jungle—and found the whole experience to be most exhilarating. Later on at a party I achieved another first, when I met a man from the Malayan Broadcasting Company. I was talking to him about my impressions of Singapore and Malaya, both past and present, and he invited me to talk on his radio station about what I had told him. It was the first time I had done such a thing, and although I made copious notes, I found that once I sat down behind the glass screen with a microphone in front of me that my mind went blank. I sat there and talked for fifteen minutes completely off the top of my head. One evening in the officer's mess at Changi, someone turned on the radio and I heard my story being broadcast, which thankfully sounded fine and everyone enjoyed it.

From Singapore I made a brief stop in the Philippines, where I spent some time with the American forces, before finally moving onto Hong Kong. This was the place that I was looking forward to seeing more than any other, after an absence of what was now nearly thirteen years. I landed at Kai Tak Aerodrome in what was known as the New Territories, in the middle of a stormy Sunday afternoon. There was nobody to meet me there, and so I made my way over to the airport buildings as quickly as I could with all my baggage. I was soon met, though, and given a very good room within the officer's mess, which was accompanied by a great deal of hospitality. It was all very nice, but I was anxious to go back and look at Hong Kong, so at the soonest possible opportunity I got a bus down to the Star Ferry to make the crossing over to the island.

Standing on that ferry brought back many memories, and I felt like I was going back home. When the ferry had docked I then walked up to the offices of the *South East China Morning Post*, where I had first opened the United Press office in 1935. Everything seemed to be exactly the same, and I went in and took the lift up to the office where I had sat all those years ago. The United Press man there, Jack James, was not at his desk because he was taking time off that Sunday afternoon. So I made my way to the

Hong Kong Hotel, which had been a favourite place of Marie and I. I was disappointed to find that it was no longer there, and had been replaced by a rather garish amusement arcade. Down the road, however, at the Gloucester Hotel, there was still a restaurant on the ground floor, and I was delighted when one of the head boys there recognised me straight away.

On the following day the weather improved, and so I went back to the offices of the *South East China Morning Post*. There I met up with a lot of people who I had known before, including Stuart Grey, who was the editor of the paper, and Percy Franklin, the general manager. They made me feel tremendously welcome, and took me out to lunch, after which I went for a walk around the places that were once so familiar. I went up to Garden Road and stood outside our old accommodation for such a long time that a lady came out and asked me what I wanted. I explained myself, and she told me that it was no longer a school quarter, but accommodation for one of the military police.

There seemed, though, to be changes all over. One of the most striking was the new National Bank of China, which had formerly been the communist Chinese Bank. I found out that the manager of the National Bank of China was a man called George Kwok, who I had previously known as the manager of the communist bank. He was a man with good connections, and I decided to go and see him. After a certain amount of haggling on the ground floor, I managed to get myself a meeting with George Kwok. We chatted for some time, and I asked him if there was any chance of me being able to visit China. He did not think it would be a problem, and made a few phone calls, before telling me that I would have to wait a couple of days. Unfortunately nothing came of this, because another United Press man had been out sailing and accidentally crossed into Chinese waters. As result, they had been suspicious about his motives, and did not welcome any more United Press men at that time.

I was determined, though, to try and get a glimpse of China, and went to see George Moss, who I had known previously when we lived in Hong Kong, and was now a police superintendent. He was able to take me right up to the border, where it was possible to look across at the communist Chinese soldiers patrolling up and down. Standing there reminded me of the time before when I had visited the border, and we had been in fear of a Japanese invasion; in some ways it seemed that things had hardly changed at all. I also went to see an RAF radar station that supposedly operated twenty-four hours a day, though I found out that this was not actually true. The twenty-four hour vigilance was maintained only up to Friday nights. This was a funny situation—apparently both sides of the border had an agreement between them that on a Friday night the radar was stopped so that the Chinese and RAF could have a night off!

The time had now come for me to go home to London, and there was a flight available carrying soldiers back to start their leave. In those days they used to take troops on chartered flights, as opposed to troop ships, and they all wore civilian clothes. At the same time I found out that the de Havilland Comet, the fastest civilian aircraft at that time, was also leaving Singapore for London. I thought that if I could get a flight on this plane it would make a terrific story, so I made enquiries and found out that the plane was fully booked until it reached Calcutta, making it possible for me to join the flight in India.

I went back to the military and asked if their plane would be stopping at Calcutta, which it was, and so I told them that I would join the Comet at that stage. My plan went ahead, but when our plane arrived in Calcutta, I was told that my seat on the Comet had been taken by a V.I.P. So I had to return to my original flight, and was very disappointed to have missed out on this opportunity. We had to spend the night in Calcutta in The Great Eastern Hotel, sleeping on camp beds, before getting up the following day to resume our journey. It was then that we heard the terrible news that the Comet had met with disaster over India. Once I was over the shock, I was thankful for having had such a lucky escape. Then it suddenly occurred to me that the United Press in London would think I was on the flight, and so I quickly phoned our local correspondent to pass on the news that I was safe and well.

When I returned to London I had lots of stories to tell about what I had seen, but everyone seemed to be preoccupied with the Coronation of Queen Elizabeth II, and also with the British Expedition that had conquered Mount Everest. My old friend Patrick Maitland was still promoting the Commonwealth of Nations, which after the unrest I had seen on my travels, seemed now to be even more important.

I was rather surprised then to receive an invitation from the government of Sudan to attend the opening of their first parliament. The United

Press was more than happy for me to go, and I spent about ten days in the Middle East, after which time I returned back home. Soon after my return I suffered a bout of illness, and was diagnosed as having heart trouble. I do not know whether it was the heat in the Middle East that caused the problem, but a doctor told me that I needed to rest for quite a long time, which I then proceeded to do.

I was finally able to get back to work early in 1956, when the big news was the "Suez Crisis," the outcome of which seemed to leave Britain isolated from the rest of the world. This was disastrous for Patrick Maitland's Commonwealth of Nations, and to compound his difficulties, he got into trouble with the Conservative Party for not voting with the party line over Suez. As a result, the party whip removed him, forcing him to become an independent member of parliament; at the next general election he lost his seat.

I think that 1956 shattered a lot of my dreams, not only in politics, but also in my interest in news coverage. It seemed to me that communications were outstripping the whole idea of news coverage, and there were great masses and volumes of words being used that did not get to the bottom of a story. Young men were coming into the profession with new ideas, and I gradually started to get the impression that the old ideas that I had followed and believed in were no longer considered to be any good. I started to lose heart in the job I had done now for almost twenty-five years. Along with all the problems I had suffered with my health, it seemed that my time in the news service was coming to an end, and I started to look forward to my retirement.

Harold Guard with John Tring in 1970 in the back garden of his retirement bungalow at Friars Cliff, Nr Christchurch, Dorset, UK. The place where many stories of the Pacific War were retold and recorded. *Author collection*

Epilogue

M y grandfather retired in 1959, and went with my grandmother
Marie to live in a little town called Friars Cliff on the south
coast of England, where he remained until his death at the age
of eighty-seven. They spent many happy years there, in spite of him suffering from failing eyesight, which in the end left him almost totally blind.
The United Press gave him a television as a retirement present with a
plaque that read, "A window on the world for one of its most famous and
finest foreign correspondents." My grandfather would always keep in touch
with world affairs, and by drawing on his own experiences, was often able
to add some insight to the stories he would hear. Even as his eyesight
worsened, he would sit close up to the television, side on, using the remaining peripheral vision he had, or listen to the radio to make sure that
he was not missing out on the latest news.

My own memories of him are mainly from when I was a small boy
and teenager, and of course, the stories that he had to tell. Even though
these tales of being in the jungle or taking part in bombing missions were
very entertaining to me, I did not really understand their significance until
later on in life. Since I began preparing this book, I've discovered additional
stories from his tapes and papers that I did not know about or had forgot-

ten, all of which has been quite a revelation for me. He would often show me some of the artefacts and photos he had collected from his naval and newspaper career, which were consigned to a black metal trunk in his garage (as my grandmother seemed to not want them in their bungalow), and these things, along with his cassette tapes, have never left my mind. I sometimes wonder if he showed them to me in the hope that I would someday write his book, as he knew that the time for him to do it himself had long since passed.

Why he never wrote the book himself, I do not know, but the task of bringing together all the various parts of his legacy has been a lengthy one, and one which he may not have felt up to, having spent many years of reporting, at times from dangerous and terrifying places. In amongst his belongings there were also many letters that had been written to him from the relatives of people fighting in the Far East, thanking him for providing them with up-to-date and detailed information about the conflicts in which their loved ones were involved. It must have been extremely touching for him to receive these. They were kept in amongst other formal accolades, such as the Asiatic-Pacific Service ribbon that was awarded to him by General MacArthur, and the letter of good wishes from Lord Mountbatten after my grandfather had his heart trouble.

This demonstrates, I believe, his values—the most important part of his stories were the people that he met, whether they were Gibson, the Papuan native boy, the Sharif of Beihan or General MacArthur himself. All of them seem to have equal standing and importance, and it may be that my grandfather's sense of humility and character are what enabled him to ingratiate himself to others and allow him, at times, to get the scoop or exclusive interview. I remember that he also had a tremendous sense of humour and the ability to make people laugh, a quality I hope has been demonstrated in his observations within this story. Harold Guard was admired and well thought of by many people. His tales are a legacy that my family has enjoyed for many years, and I hope that you have too.

—*John Tring*

Index